THE ETHICS OF
JOURNALISM

THE ETHICS OF
JOURNALISM

BY

NELSON ANTRIM CRAWFORD

Head of the Department of Industrial Journalism
Kansas State Agricultural College

GREENWOOD PRESS, PUBLISHERS
NEW YORK

Originally purchased in 1924
by Alfred A. Knopf

First Greenwood Reprinting 1969

SBN 8371-2155-8

TO
MY FATHER
AND
MY MOTHER

PREFACE

It is a truism that no human institution is more potent, for the good or the evil of society, than the press. It is of the utmost importance, therefore, not alone to journalists, but to the general public as well, that its standards of practice shall be such as to further the best interests of society.

This book is an attempt to stimulate the formation, development, and acceptance of such standards. It seeks to present the contemporary status of the press and the reasons therefor, not theoretically but realistically. While the writer nowhere hesitates to state his own views or the views of others, he does not offer them as the final word on the subjects under discussion, but rather as stimuli to independent thinking on the part of the reader. The function of the volume is not to lay down a series of rules for the guidance of the young journalist, but rather to aid him in formulating for himself an ethical philosophy of his profession that will be realistic, discerning, intellectually honest, and applicable to the press as a social institution. When a sufficient proportion of the members of any profession hold and act upon such philosophies, that profession has, potentially at least, achieved its social salvation.

Throughout the book, as will be observed, extensive reference is made to other writings on journalism and to specific practices of newspapers. In some instances, passages of considerable length are quoted for the benefit of those to whom the sources are not easily accessible. The book may thus be read rapidly as a unit, by individuals or by classes in which a limited time is devoted to the ethical problems of journalism; or it may be used as the basic text for a term or semester course in the subject, the several subtopics being elaborated through use of the reference material indicated.

The writer is grateful for the innumerable suggestions, from sources known and unknown, which have aided him in the preparation of the book. In particular, he is indebted to many practicing journalists and teachers of journalism. The suggestions of Dr. J. W. Cunliffe, Director of the School of Journalism, Columbia University, and of Dr. M. L. Spencer, Director of the School of Journalism, University of Washington, have been of special value. He acknowledges with thanks the courtesy of the several authors and publishers who have given him the privilege of quotation, and of *The Nation, The Washington Newspaper,* and *Mental Hygiene,* which have kindly permitted the use of portions of articles originally written by him for these publications.

NELSON ANTRIM CRAWFORD.

CONTENTS

THE ETHICS OF JOURNALISM

I

THE BUSINESS ETHICS OF PUBLISHING

A newspaper, obviously, is a commodity. Copies of newspapers are bought and sold. Advertisers pay, reluctantly or gladly, large sums of money for the privilege of publishing advertising in them.

The newspaper, if soundly and legitimately run, has no substantial sources of income other than its circulation and its advertising. Here and there are country newspapers which are unsoundly run in that the job printing done by the publisher serves to cover a deficit run up through the operation of the newspaper. Here and there are newspapers, still fewer in number, which accept or even solicit contributions from individuals, corporations, or political parties as compensation for assistance which the publisher gives. The great majority of American newspapers, however, are outside these small categories. The typical American newspaper derives its income from circulation and from advertising, except for the relatively insignificant sums obtained through the sale of waste newsprint and similar items.

So far, the newspaper is a commercial enterprise. Persons who look at the press from this point of view refer to publishing as "the newspaper business," just as the colt-like young reporter refers to it as the "newspaper game." Regarded as a commercial enterprise, the newspaper owes to the persons directly concerned, the adver-

3

tisers and the subscribers or buyers, the same obligations that are owed by any other commercial enterprise, modified only by the inherent differences between the newspaper and other such enterprises.

The subscriber, when he takes the paper, is entitled to know what he is getting. No solicitor or other person connected with a newspaper has any right to make any misrepresentations concerning the paper, concerning a premium offered by it, or concerning any other factor involved in the transaction. If the newspaper is to maintain the standards of ordinary business, it cannot follow the old legal motto, *Caveat emptor,* any more than the enlightened merchant can follow this motto with reference to goods sold in his establishment. It is too much to expect that the solicitor or newsdealer shall be able to discuss with nicety the fine points of the news, the features, and the editorial policy of the paper. He can, however, in a general way, present the paper as it is. Few papers intentionally misrepresent to prospective subscribers the quality of their product. Where misrepresentation in solicitation takes place, it is commonly due to the ignorance or dishonesty of the solicitor.

Once the subscription has been obtained, the newspaper is under obligation to see that the publication reaches the subscriber promptly and regularly, and to furnish the edition which is most satisfactory as to news contained, time of delivery, and other factors. All substantial newspapers make an effort to fulfil these obligations. They are a part not only of ethics but of ordinary business policy.

In the case of the large metropolitan dailies, which are in a small minority among American newspapers although they have the largest circulations, subscriptions are frequently a minor factor. The newspaper is sold from day to day and persons become the equivalent of subscribers by their habit of constant buying rather than by the fact of having their names enrolled on the books of the paper. The obligation of the newspaper to these persons is nevertheless the same.

Some large newspapers refuse to sell extra copies which they suspect are to be used for propaganda purposes. In at least one office, there is a rule that a request for twenty or more copies must be referred to the general manager, who investigates the reason for the request. The basis of such rules goes back to the time when certain newspapers and magazines were subsidized by corporations or individuals, the method being the purchase of great numbers of extra copies containing material laudatory of the subsidizers. Many persons today believe that newspapers are extensively subsidized; and their belief is strengthened if, for example, they receive from a railroad company a marked copy of a newspaper containing an editorial defending the railroads. The public would be unable to believe that the editorial was sincere and published with no expectation of reward. For this reason the newspaper would be wholly justified in refusing to sell any copies to the railroad company. It would thus avoid even the appearance of evil. While it is sometimes argued in opposition to this point of view that the company could reprint the editorial and circulate it, this would not be true if the newspaper were copyrighted, as is the case with a large proportion of metropolitan dailies.

In building its circulation a newspaper has also certain obligations to the advertiser, because, from a financial standpoint, its primary purpose in building circulation is to obtain a higher rate for advertising. To the metropolitan daily, deriving at least eighty per cent of its revenue from advertising, and receiving from circulation less than enough money to pay its white paper bills, additional circulation means actual financial loss unless the advertising rate can be increased. Smaller newspapers, which are able to make a profit on subscriptions, nevertheless reckon the advertising revenue added by increase in circulation as the more important factor.

Obviously, the manner in which the circulation has been built will be of significance to the advertiser. The subscriber who is taking the paper because a young woman friend has asked him to subscribe in order that she may win votes toward an automobile or a piano, will not have the same interest in it that will be manifested by a subscriber who takes the paper only because he likes to read it. The housewife who subscribes for a newspaper in order to secure a set of silverware offered as a premium does not, by reason of that fact, become an interested reader. Her interest in the paper, it may be assumed, varies inversely with the value of the premium. If, as sometimes happens, the premium proves to have been misrepresented, the silverware, for instance, turning out to be brass, there is introduced into the transaction a factor calculated to make the subscriber not merely indifferent but perhaps actually hostile to the paper.

While, except in case of actual misrepresentation, neither the contest nor the premium plan can be condemned as contrary to sound ethics, the fact remains that the publication which abstains from both plays somewhat more fairly with its advertisers. This is true even though the advertisers, under modern methods of circulation statements and audits, know in just what way circulation is obtained.

The fundamental ethical obligation of the newspaper to the advertiser is, of course, not to misrepresent its circulation. It cannot be emphasized too often that the advertiser buys space not simply as space but as an opportunity to address the readers of the paper.

Honest circulation figures are a development of recent years. Not long ago publishers expressed resentment at the suggestion on the part of advertisers or advertising agents that dependable circulation figures should be presented and that these should be subject to verification by disinterested parties. The first attempt to give circulation figures at all was made by George P. Rowell, who published the first issue of his *American Newspaper Directory* in 1870. The newspaper situation of the day is shown by the fact that nine years later he was forced to resort to a key in giving circulation ratings. In some cases the key allowed for a variation of 50,000 in circulation, although Mr. Rowell expressed the hope that it would "work more entirely to the satisfaction of all persons interested" than the former plan of publishing actual figures. In his 1879 directory, he made the following statement:

"In 1870, when it was first decided to give information on this subject, the editor applied to proprietors of newspapers for statements, and inserted before the figures so obtained the word 'claims.' After a time objections were urged against this word, and to avoid its use, publishers offered to prove reports, by affidavits and otherwise. Many, however, were satisfied with the word as used, and arguing that one claim was as good as another, set up pretensions which could not be substantiated. It became evident that if the book was to become an authority the 'claimed' circulations would have to be excluded. Thenceforth, those newspapers whose proprietors offered proof had their circulation figures given *positively*, without any preliminary word; in all other cases the figures were followed by the word 'estimated.'

"In the course of a year or two the word 'estimated' became

as objectionable as the other, and newspaper publishers frequently asked that it be omitted. To this request, the response was uniformly made that the word could only be omitted in those cases where an offer to prove correctness accompanied the circulation statement when given.

"This position gave offense to many. It was a system introduced for the protection of honest publishers against their more unscrupulous neighbors. It seemed a good one when it was adopted. It doubtless answered an excellent purpose in its time, but it finally gave rise to so much dissatisfaction that it was abandoned.

"A statement, in detail, of the number issued is now all that is required, and this may be made in any form which suits the convenience of the publisher furnishing it. If notoriously false, it is likely to be disregarded, and, in any event, is liable to receive the critical scrutiny of rivals capable of bringing to bear much positive knowledge on the subject." [1]

Largely through the demands of advertisers and advertising agencies, the situation with reference to circulation figures has been steadily bettered. The most potent force in this direction has been the Audit Bureau of Circulations, a non-profit making corporation, comprising publishers, advertisers, and advertising agents. The A. B. C., as it is popularly called, has formulated and adopted a definition of "net paid circulation" and has also devised a plan whereby the publisher's figures are subjected to independent audit. This insures that all publications belonging to the bureau may be compared on the basis of a common system of rating. Since practically all large newspapers belong to the bureau, misrepresentation of quantity of circulation has been substantially eliminated, so far as the stronger publications are concerned.

[1] Preface, *American Newspaper Directory*, 1879.

In a recent editorial convention, however, the writer heard a country newspaper man seriously ask the question whether actual circulation or claimed circulation should be the basis of certain plans under discussion. The fact that circulation on the smaller papers is frequently misrepresented (though not to the same extent as formerly) is one of the chief reasons why these publications receive but little national advertising. Not a few country publishers are still giving the number of copies printed as the actual circulation.

Aside from quantity of circulation, the advertiser or advertising agent must consider quality; that is, he must take into account the buying power and disposition of the persons to whom the paper goes. There is no fixed standard by which to measure quality of circulation, nor would it be practicable to apply such measurement if it existed. It obviously would be impossible to ascertain the income and the wants of every subscriber for a metropolitan daily. The measurement of quality is necessarily somewhat intangible. In soliciting advertising, the newspaper is under obligation to misrepresent in no way the quality of its circulation. Its obligation is to present accurate, unbiased data and to draw honest conclusions therefrom. Any one examining the promotion material sent out by newspapers and magazines, however, cannot fail to suspect that there is exaggeration in the claims of quality circulation. The obligation to maintain accuracy in such claims, however, is generally recognized, at least in theory.

A further obligation rests upon newspapers to exercise no discrimination among advertisers. This does not mean that special rates charged for special positions, or for special types of advertising, or on long-time contracts, are not wholly ethical. It means simply that between two advertisers of the same type of business, utilizing the same amount of space for the same number of insertions, there should be no discrimination as to position or price. It is an application of the one-price principle that has transformed business in the United States from a bargaining basis.

Censorship of advertising arouses perhaps a wider variety of opinions than does any other ethical problem involved in publishing as a business. Like honesty in circulation claims, honesty in advertising is a modern development. The advertiser has been honest no longer than the publisher. Indeed, the growth of honesty in advertising has been stimulated largely by newspaper publishers. The standards of advertising, especially among the large advertisers, are higher than ever before, and are notably higher in this country than in other countries at the present time.

There are still, however, some advertisers who are intentionally dishonest, and others who mislead through excessive enthusiasm, carelessness, or the mistakes of employees. State laws against fraudulent advertising have never worked with thorough effectiveness. The public, being inexpert in merchandising, can be protected against such advertisers most effectively by the publications which carry advertising. Nevertheless, there is a wide variation in the standards of advertising practice enforced by newspapers. At one end of the scale are those publishers, now few in number, who will accept any advertising which will go through the mails and sometimes some which will not. The foreign-language press is, on the whole, the most flagrant example of that tendency in the United States.[1] At the other end are those who exercise a strict censorship

[1] For statistical data, see Park, *The Immigrant Press and its Control*, pp. 369–373.

upon the advertising columns, excluding in block all advertising of certain undesirable classes, such as patent medicines and speculative stocks, and scrutinizing carefully all other advertising submitted.

In some cases the advertising is specifically guaranteed. This practice is less common on newspapers than on periodicals, but the guaranty of a newspaper, when made, is likely to be more iron-bound than that of a magazine. The practice of guaranteeing advertising originated with *The Farm Journal* (Philadelphia) in 1880. In the newspaper field it came into prominence with the militant campaign of *The New York Tribune* against fraudulent advertising, begun in 1914. The financial argument against the guaranty plan, sometimes heard, is not borne out by facts. The actual cost of refunds to customers by a newspaper operating under the plan is not likely to exceed one-fifth of one per cent of the advertising revenue. The plan has been employed successfully in small towns as well as in larger cities.

It is often supposed that an advertising guaranty is maintained solely in the interest of the readers. This is not the case. The honest and scrupulous advertiser feels justly that the value of his advertising is diminished if advertising by dishonest or questionable merchants is permitted in the same paper. A specific guaranty enhances the value of all advertising in the paper. If the advertiser knows in advance, as he should be told, all types of advertising accepted by the newspaper, and then inserts his advertisement, he probably has no sound moral justification in complaining of the quality of advertising which the newspaper publishes. From the larger standpoint of service as the basis of business, strict censorship of advertising—with guaranty—on the part of the publisher in the interest of the advertiser, even without considering that of the public, is thoroughly to be commended.

On the other hand, no publisher has any ethical justification for refusing to publish advertising on the sole ground that it competes with the advertising now running in his paper, that it is objectionable for other reasons to some advertiser, or that it is objectionable to the publisher himself, personally. For example, it is wholly unjustifiable for a publisher to sell to a single hardware store the exclusive right to advertise hardware through his paper. The newspapers which declined to run the advertising of Samuel Hopkins Adams's novel, *The Clarion,* apparently because they were receiving a large advertising revenue from the patent medicine business which Mr. Adams attacked, showed themselves lacking in the ethical principles of ordinary business. The publisher is justified in refusing advertising devoted to attacks upon a competitor of the advertiser, and must, for safety's sake, decline it if it is libelous. On the other hand, there is no justification for a newspaper which publishes so-called publicity advertising representing one side of a controversy, to refuse to publish similar publicity advertising setting forth the opposite side. The moral obligation of the merchant to sell goods to whoever applies for them has been written into law in many places. A similar obligation, although not covered by statute, exists with reference to the newspaper and advertising.

While, as has been pointed out, modern business is based upon the principle of service, no obligation rests upon the newspaper to give to the advertiser any special service, such as investigating markets or aiding the advertiser to obtain distribution of his commodity in the community in which the newspaper circulates. Such activities are perfectly proper on the part of a newspaper, but they rest upon ethical obligation no more than does the case of the dry goods merchant who maintains a rest room as a service to his women customers.

Again, there seems to be no specific obligation on the part of a newspaper to refuse advertising which it is convinced will not pay a profit if run in the particular newspaper concerned. Some few newspapers, notably *The Chicago Tribune,* have adopted this policy for the purpose of promoting the general cause of advertising by making all advertising profitable.

It is still insufficiently recognized that the sale of advertising space is a commercial transaction, in which the advertiser pays a reasonable sum for the privilege of addressing the readers of the paper in a space of given dimensions. Neither legally nor morally is he entitled to any more than this space or to any special privileges to be extended by the publisher.

Publishing as a business is comparatively young, and there remains a hang-over from the old days when it was a hand-to-mouth trade. It must be remembered that the agate line, as a standard of advertising measurement, was adopted little more than thirty years ago, even on the largest papers. There is consequently a tradition of irregular rates in the mind of the public, including advertisers. Moreover, and still worse, there is a tradition of advertising as a form of charity to the starving printer, or a contribution to avert blackmail, to purchase support in the columns of the newspaper, or at best to help maintain the press, recognized as a desirable institution. These attitudes are found in their frankest form in the smaller places, but points of view based fundamentally upon them are common even in metropolitan centers.

In line with these facts, the merchant in the small town may insist on a free news story whenever he gets in his season's stock, or the banker may call upon the publisher to print as an editorial "canned" material issued by a partisan political agency. A monument company advertising for salesmen, writes: "Should we decide to place this ad. in your paper, we would expect you, in your local news column, to give us a boost and do your best to help our ad. secure the man we want." The theaters and motion picture houses are so insistent on free newspaper publicity that many publishers charge them a higher advertising rate than they charge other industries. While the excess allows for the supposedly free copy that is published, the practice is obviously a most undesirable business practice, even though it be assumed—as is not always true —that the reader recognizes the free "puffs" and distinguishes them from legitimate news. In the larger cities, news involving large stores or their owners is sometimes suppressed at the request, or even without the request, of the advertisers. At present this is less common than is popularly supposed, and less common, moreover, than was formerly the case.

It was less than twenty years ago that patent medicine advertisers were inserting in their contracts with publishers a clause making the contracts voidable if any laws restricting the sale of patent medicines were passed, or if any matter prejudicial to the interests of the medicine manufacturer appeared in the paper. In response to demands from the advertisers, newspapers in many parts of the United States requested the legislatures to kill bills providing for the publication of the formulae of patent medicines, and in one state the Press Association passed a resolution

opposing such a bill and appointed a committee to fight it.[1]
Many newspaper readers, having known of this situation
in 1904 and 1905, suppose that it still exists.

The increasing tendency of newspapers is to disregard
the demands of advertisers in such matters, only partly,
it is true, on ethical grounds, partly for purely commercial
reasons. Not only is it considered bad policy to permit an
advertiser to gain the impression that he "owns the paper,"
but an accession to one advertiser's request brings scores
of similar requests from other advertisers; while, on the
other hand, the publication of matter unfavorable to an
advertiser pleases his competitors. From an ethical standpoint, the publisher who conforms to the demands of advertisers is cheating his readers, as will be pointed out in
greater detail further on, and at the same time he is not
playing fair with those advertisers who have purchased their
space as a business transaction. Indeed, under these
circumstances, no advertiser can be sure, no matter how
much free publicity and other illegitimate service he receives, that he is obtaining for his money the same value
that other advertisers receive.

The competent and honest newspaper man meets requests of this sort with a courteous but firm refusal, ex-
plaining the position of the paper and not infrequently
convincing the advertiser. Where the advertiser goes to
the extent of withdrawing his advertising, a public explanation in the columns of the newspaper is both ethical and
useful. The Enid (Oklahoma) *Eagle*, a daily in a town
of less than twenty thousand people, performed this
function courageously early in 1922, when motion picture
theaters withdrew their advertising. The published comment of *The Eagle* follows:

[1] Adams, *The Great American Fraud*, pp. 163–164.

"Meeting of theater owners was held in Enid Sunday and decision reached to withhold all advertising patronage from *The Eagle,* according to announcement Monday morning.

"Reason for the action is said to be because *The Eagle* has not suppressed news concerning the immoral doings of movie people, nor kept out of its columns news of the local movement to close the picture shows on Sundays. Particular umbrage is said to have been taken by the theater owners because of an article concerning that distinguished low-brow, Fat Arbuckle, which appeared in the paper Sunday morning.

"The theater owners are well within their rights in withdrawing patronage from *The Eagle.* It has never been the policy of *The Eagle* to permit movie show proprietors to dictate its attitude on questions of public morals, nor to censor *The Eagle's* news columns.

"The local profession, through some misconception of the rights they imagine an advertiser is entitled to, has almost constantly in the past endeavored to dictate the policy of *The Eagle* concerning every question affecting picture shows and vaudeville. Withdrawal of their patronage from the paper was inevitable."

The Eagle also published a list of the demands made upon it by theater proprietors:

"Suppress news of movements aimed to result in Sunday closing.

"Don't publish complaints of patrons who have felt insulted by indecencies on the stage.

"Use personal influence and the influence of the paper with the mayor to forestall movie legislation.

"Suppress stories showing why the City Censorship Board cannot function.

"Suppress news of activities of the Parent-Teachers' Association, working for cleaner shows.

"Reject all news matter or Forum communications which might be detrimental to the theatres.

"Support candidates for city offices who are endorsed by the theatre owners.

"Write editorials against proposed increases in theatre licenses.

"Suppress news of epidemics, lest the box office receipts of the theatres suffer.

"Print free reading notices and run free cuts with every advertisement.

"Print regularly a portion of the propaganda sent out by press agents of movie stars, which in reality is nothing but thinly veiled advertising.

"Solicit 'co-operative' advertising from other lines of business to be banked around a free advertisement of special attractions in return for one paid ad.

"Suppress news of patrons being bitten by rats or having their furs chewed up by rats while attending a movie."

A similar situation, involving a somewhat more subtle appeal on the part of advertisers to a newspaper, was appropriately handled by *The Chicago Tribune*. A letter, from the representatives of an advertiser seeking political influence in return for the advertising, was published in the correspondence department of the newspaper. On the same page appeared the editorial reply of the newspaper. The letter follows:

"Chicago, Sept. 2.—For several years past your publication has been among those consistently favored with a substantial share of the advertising appropriations of the National Kellastone Company, America's largest producer of magnesite products.

"Doubtless you look upon this advertising account as mighty desirable business, and we feel that therefore you will be interested in learning that under the contemplated tariff on magnesite which is now before the conference committee at Washington, the source of this advertising is seriously threatened with extinction.

"In other words, should the magnesite tariff in its present form be adopted, the business of the National Kellastone Company and of all other concerns dealing in or handling domestic magnesite or its products, will be seriously impaired because of the impossibility of competing in price with foreign magnesite, which, under the new tariff, could be delivered to American seaports at figures which American concerns cannot meet and exist.

"If you have followed the tariff conferences you probably are aware that in the original Fordney tariff bill, a tariff of $10 per ton on crude, and $15 per ton on calcined magnesite of foreign production was placed on this product. This tariff was entirely satisfactory to the American interests concerned, and the bill was duly passed by the house and sent to the senate.

"Meanwhile, importers of foreign magnesite, and representatives of foreign exporters of this product, brought strong influences to bear, with the result that the senate reduced the proposed tariff to $6.25 on crude and $12.50 on calcined magnesite imports.

"Immediately, representatives of American producers appeared before the senate committee, presenting facts and figures to substantiate their claims to the justness of the original tariff. Their pleas were unavailing, however, and the bill, carrying the lower tariff, was turned over to the conference committee, where it now awaits final action.

"Now, as we have already pointed out, should this lower tariff be passed, its adoption means the closing down of many American concerns engaged in the magnesite business. In fact, foreign competition has long been a thorn in the side of this industry. It has already caused the discontinuance of many American magnesite mines whose owners could not pay American wages and American freight rates, and still successfully meet the prices on foreign products.

"The labor employed in the American magnesite industry is among the best paid in the country, and ideal working conditions are maintained. The foreign magnesite which comes to our shores, however, is the product of the cheapest character of labor, produced under miserable conditions, with wages equivalent to about 1 cent per day American money.

"As far as fair and square competition of a foreign source is concerned, American interests have no quarrel. They are perfectly willing that there should be competition, provided it is on a just and equitable basis—provided it is not permitted to prosper at the cost of destruction to an American industry representing millions invested and employing many thousands of American workmen at good American wages.

"Therefore, as the American magnesite producers are seeking only a fair fighting chance for existence; and as your publication, an influential factor in the thought of the nation, can do much on the side of fair play, we are writing to urge your endorsement of these claims and to bespeak your cooperation and support in this endeavor to cause the adoption of the higher tariff as provided in the original Fordney bill.

"A letter to your senators and congressmen, in behalf of our client, the National Kellastone Company, and of the industry in general, requesting passage of the original bill will, we are quite hopeful, be of the desired effect, and preserve to our mutual benefit this industry which, although quite large, is still in its infancy.

"Simmonds and Simmonds,
"Per F. M. Simmonds."

This is the editorial answer:

"A THREAT AND AN ANSWER

"A lengthy letter from Simmonds & Simmonds, an advertising agency, appearing in the Voice of the People today, speaks for itself, in a manner to which newspapers are more or less accustomed, but in a tone less diplomatic and in words more direct than usual. In effect it threatens us with the penalty of withdrawal of advertising if we refuse to work for a high protective tariff on magnesite.

"It says we have been consistently 'favored' with certain advertising appropriations. We might remark truthfully that use of advertising appropriations to place advertisements before *Tribune* readers is no more of a 'favor' to this newspaper than *The Tribune's* acceptance and publication of such advertisements is a 'favor' to the advertiser. It is a plain business proposition assuring value received on both sides. But that is beside the point.

"The issue is whether we should 'favor' an industry, regardless of its effect upon the country at large, merely to advance our private interests, and under threat. That is the log rolling method of building tariff schedules and one of which we disapprove. The questions of whether the duty on magnesite should be $10 a ton or $6.25 a ton, of whether the smaller duty will put certain American industries out of profitable business, and of whether the effect of foreign competition will be good or bad for the country in general, are independent questions to be studied and answered by the proper authorities. But they should be decided on their merits, not upon any weight of special influence directed according to the immediate financial returns to those exercising such influence.

"A newspaper which bases its policy on any such influence or is actuated by any such motives is as false to its constituency as a congressman who accepts money for his vote. This newspaper does not and will not conduct either its advertising or its editorial departments in that way."

A better statement of the function of a newspaper in connection with advertising could hardly be made.

The stand taken by the publishers quoted is obviously the only ethical stand that can be taken in fairness to both readers and advertisers in general. There is possibly no obligation on the part of a newspaper to publish an account of such a controversy; one's judgment in that matter would depend on one's definition of news. In the opinion of the writer, matter of this character is news of interest and significance to readers. Moreover, discussion of the problem is educative to both advertisers and readers, many of whom have never faced the issue involved.

Whether or not publication of the data is made, the fact remains that in few cases can advertisers afford to stay out of a profitable advertising medium for any considerable time. Although there are numerous newspapers in Boston, a boycott of *The Evening Transcript* in the summer of 1920 by a group of shoe concerns because the paper published the facts about the shoe market, ended after seven weeks. In not a few cases, readers have told merchants that they would withdraw their patronage unless advertising were published in their favorite newspapers. Where a newspaper is unable to withstand an attack by advertisers, it is weak in either financial backing or editorial prestige, commonly in both.

It is of course wholly justifiable, and in some cases ethically necessary, to reject advertising which may cause suspicion on the part of readers that other than a strictly commercial transaction is involved. An instance of this, which occurred in 1897, when newspapers generally maintained lower standards than they do now, is related by Elmer Davis,[1] of *The New York Times:*

"Some months later all the regular advertising of the city government was unexpectedly offered to *The Times.* This amounted to about $150,000 a year, a sum which would have made a tremendous difference to *The Times* of that period.

[1] *History of the New York Times,* pp. 221–223.

Moreover, assurances were brought to the management of the paper by a gentleman who was a friend both of the publisher and of the Tammany leaders that this offer was made with absolutely no strings. It was neither the expectation nor the desire of Tammany that *The Times* should feel itself influenced in any way, and it was understood that the allotment of the advertising did not in any way involve a modification of *The Times's* general hostility to Tammany in local politics. The only reason for this sudden windfall, said the gentleman who brought the news, was the conviction of the Tammany leaders that it was a good thing for the general interests of the Democratic Party to have a conservative Democratic paper maintained in New York City. That paper's feelings about Tammany did not enter into the case.

"The publisher of *The Times* had entire confidence in the good faith of the gentleman who gave him these assurances, and saw no need for questioning the good faith of the Tammany leaders. But whether or not their intentions were honorable, their proposal was unacceptable. It was asking too much of human nature to suppose that thereafter when *The Times* had reason to attack Tammany, as it certainly would (its exposures of graft payments for gambling-house protection were not very far in the future), the subconscious, if not the conscious minds of those in *The Times* office might be affected by the thought that $150,000 was at stake. By that time the paper might have got accustomed to living on a higher scale, and would have missed the $150,000 more than if it had never had it. Moreover, *The Times* was still far behind its rivals in circulation. If this considerable revenue were suddenly awarded to the smallest in circulation of New York morning papers, everybody would believe that Tammany had bought *The Times,* no matter how pure the motives of the organization or of the paper's management. The shadow was as bad as the substance, in this case; from any point of view the offer was unacceptable."

It is sometimes argued by critics of the press that the comparatively small lineage of advertising carried by the advanced liberal and the radical press is due to advertisers' personal opposition to liberal and radical views. The conservative paper receives advertising, these critics believe, because of conformity to the advertiser's opinions. Thus the conclusion is reached that financial success in publishing is attainable only through subservience to the demands of advertisers.

The fact of the matter is less simple. Among the factors that produce a successful advertising medium is not only buying power but buying disposition on the part of its readers. The readers of many of the radical journals do not possess, in the opinion of advertisers, sufficient buying power to justify the advertising rate that is charged. In the case of liberal and radical publications whose readers possess high purchasing power, advertisers maintain that the buying disposition is destroyed or reduced—except for certain commodities, notably books—by the material which the paper publishes. In other words, the mood which is produced is not conducive to buying merchandise. The advertiser is interested in cash returns rather than in abstract policies. Few if any radical or liberal journals have been influenced in a conservative direction by the policies of advertisers; the newspaper or periodical of this type is usually not dependent on advertising for its support.

In general, it may be concluded that while there is not yet entire freedom on the part of newspapers from direct control by advertisers, there is an increasing tendency in this direction, especially among papers that are financially sound and that present their cases to their readers. The important factor in the entire situation is the reader. He has a sense of fair play. If the newspaper can bring this sense to bear on controversies with advertisers, there can be little question of the outcome. The maintenance of effective ethical standards in the publishing business, as elsewhere, requires not only high principle but the application of psychological laws.

Additional Readings

Adams, *The Clarion.*
Adams, *The Great American Fraud,* pp. 133–185.
Rowell, *American Newspaper Directory,* 1879, Preface.
Audit Bureau of Circulations, *Scientific Space Selection,* pp. 70–90.
Park, *The Immigrant Press and its Control,* pp. 359–411.
Davis, *History of The New York Times,* pp. 219–223, 315–322.
Moses, *The Deadhead Reading Notice.* (Pamphlet of *The New York Evening Post.*)
How Confidence Began. (Pamphlet of *The Farm Journal,* Philadelphia.)
How It Works. (Pamphlet of *The New York Tribune.*)
Lewis, *Guaranteed Advertising,* in *Bulletin of the University of Washington,* General Series No. 101, pp. 46–51.
Powell, *Building a Circulation, University of Missouri Bulletin,* Vol. 15, No. 6, pp. 10–23.
Smith, *Advertising,* in *Civilization in the United States,* pp. 381–395.

II

JOURNALISM AS A PROFESSION

Among newspaper men and the reading public, there is a general recognition that journalism is more than simply the business of publishing. It is more than merely selling a commodity. This fact has been realized more or less, not only by newspaper workers but by other classes of the population, from the earliest days of newspapers or their predecessors, the newsbooks and similar publications. The licensing laws governing the press, passed in times when licenses were not required or were required under much less strict provisions for other occupations, indicate that journalism was always recognized as having a certain public or quasi-public function.

Those few persons who in these latter days refer to newspaper work exclusively as a business do not understand its history or its generally recognized function. They are almost invariably men who have grown up in other activities and have turned to journalism as they would turn to the dry goods business, to the selling of real estate, or to any other strictly commercial occupation. These persons, it must be remembered, are relatively few, although their number is slowly increasing. They are confined, for the most part, to great metropolitan dailies, the publication of any one of which calls for an investment too large to be handled by any one but a capitalist. These great dailies are in a small minority among American newspapers, al-

25

though their greater circulations and their publication in centers of population give them a disproportionate influence.

The owners of most of the smaller newspapers are either professional newspaper men or printers. In both of these occupations there is a tradition of public accountability and public service. Likewise, the men working in all ed-itorial and writing positions on the large dailies are likely to feel strongly that the newspaper is not primarily a busi-ness enterprise but a quasi-public institution. The second-class mail rates granted to newspapers and periodicals by the government are an indication of the general conviction that newspapers exist to serve the public. The increase made in these rates a few years ago was undoubtedly due in part to a feeling that newspapers were no longer serving this interest as they should serve it. Such a feeling is erroneous. The newspapers are now serving the public interest better than they served it twenty-five, fifty, or a hundred years ago. Their service to the public has not increased as rapidly, however, as the public demand for service, the public conscience, has developed.

Practically all discussions of the newspaper, of which there are many in magazines, books, and public addresses, are founded on the assumption that the newspapers exist primarily to serve a quasi-public function. Schemes to regulate the newspaper, much more far-reaching than schemes to regulate any other occupation, are predicated upon this assumption.

When it comes to the question of what particular public or quasi-public function the newspaper is expected to serve, there is a wide difference of opinion. The newspapers are urged by some to state all the facts without fear or favor. They are besought by others to omit all news which might suggest crime to the criminal, abnormal acts to the psychopathic, or mischief to the children. One critic points to their duty to editorialize in favor of liberal or radical views, another to take a stand in favor of the Constitution as interpreted by the National Security League and similar organizations. One critic would have the newspaper sell fish, coal, or what not, in order to break local monopolies. Still another would have the newspaper devote its attention primarily to getting the good men into office and keeping out the bad.

These differences as to the proper function of the newspaper as related to the public are due, not altogether but largely, to mental confusion. It is only in recent years that the significance of facts has been recognized by anybody. It is now recognized only by a minority. In classical times there were no means of checking the credibility of evidence, even if canons of evidence had been devised. Who was there to dispute Herodotus?—or, for that matter, Julius Caesar, although the dullness of the latter's accounts would seem strong evidence of their honesty? As a matter of fact, it was only in certain exact sciences, such as geometry, that any attempt was made to establish a body of incontrovertible fact. For the rest, a system of abstract philosophy was originated. This held sway in the minds of every one down to the most recent times. It was elaborated in the Middle Ages to extremes of profundity and of absurdity. It is possible to conceive of a system of metaphysics based on observed and substantiated facts, but no such system has ever existed. Systems of metaphysics have commonly been based on tradition, on the supposed word of a god, on popular belief, or purely on the cunningly arranged plans of some theoretical thinker. According to these systems, men arrived at truth or goodness through some mysterious faculties directly or indirectly implanted in them by a creator.   St. Paul was convinced of Christ's divinity by what he conceived to be an obvious vision.   The farmers, in the opinion of Thomas Jefferson, were sagacious in public affairs because God had mystically endowed them with political wisdom.

With the immense increase in facilities for obtaining and verifying facts, and with the development of the scientific method of arriving at conclusions from definitely ascertained facts, careful thinkers have come to realize that in every avenue of life verified facts are the only sure way to dependable conclusions.   The conviction has been reached that the method which has been applied to scientific research may likewise be applied to studies in economics, sociology, and politics, the subjects with which everyday conversation and newspaper stories alike chiefly deal.   The corollary follows that conclusions based on anything less than investigation of facts stand an even chance of being wrong, and in practice, probably more than an even chance, because they will be colored by the prejudices and taboos of the race, which are themselves based largely on false rationalization.

This view of the importance of facts has the practical support of an extremely small minority, who are willing to apply it to any of the problems of life.   It has the theoretical support of a somewhat larger minority, who practically apply it only to questions on which they have no fixed opinions that they are determined firmly to hold.   It has no consideration from the vast majority, who cling to their inherited views and prejudices, precisely as their ancestors have done for untold centuries.

So little consideration has been given in the past to facts that the second minority mentioned is likely to express toward many of them the same feeling that was manifested sixty years ago and is manifested in ignorant circles today, concerning the principle of evolution. This in turn is merely a repetition of the experience of Bacon, Galileo, and other scientists, when confronting their contemporaries with facts that clashed with preconceived notions. The supposedly intelligent capitalist, the supposedly intelligent socialist, the supposedly intelligent single-taxer, is likely to admit theoretically the significance of facts, but may condemn as "immoral," "destructive," "undesirable," or "unbelievable," all facts which do not support his conclusions.

The general public, of course, shows still less intelligence. In America it clings firmly to its cherished beliefs as to the complete superiority of the United States, the immorality of the French, the barbarism of the Russians, and other fond illusions. In other countries the herd has illusions quite as fantastic, but because of a lower proportion of literacy it does not express them so conspicuously.

Trotter's statement of the situation is sound and adequate:

"In matters that really interest him, man cannot support the suspense of judgment which science so often has to enjoin. He is too anxious to feel certain to have time to know. So that we see of the sciences, mathematics appearing first, then astronomy, then physics, then chemistry, then biology, then psychology, then sociology—but always the new field was grudged to the new method, and we still have the denial to sociology of the name of science. Nowadays, matters of national defence, of politics, of religion, are still too important for knowledge, and remain subjects for certitude; that is to say, in them we still prefer the comfort of instinctive belief, because we have not learnt adequately to value the capacity to foretell.

"Direct observation of man reveals at once the fact that a

very considerable proportion of his beliefs are non-rational to a degree which is immediately obvious without any special examination, and with no special resources other than common knowledge. If we examine the mental furniture of the average man, we shall find it made up of a vast number of judgments of a very precise kind upon subjects of very great variety, complexity, and difficulty. He will have fairly settled views upon the origin and nature of the universe, and upon what he will probably call its meaning; he will have conclusions as to what is to happen to him at death and after, as to what is and what should be the basis of conduct. He will know how the country should be governed, and why it is going to the dogs, why this piece of legislation is good and that bad. He will have strong views upon military and naval strategy, the principles of taxation, the use of alcohol and vaccination, the treatment of influenza, the prevention of hydrophobia, upon municipal trading, the teaching of Greek, upon what is permissible in art, satisfactory in literature, and hopeful in science.

"The bulk of such opinions must necessarily be without rational basis, since many of them are concerned with problems admitted by the expert to be still unsolved, while as to the rest it is clear that the training and experience of no average man can qualify him to have any opinion upon them at all. The rational method adequately used would have told him that on the great majority of these questions there could be for him but one attitude—that of suspended judgment.

"In view of the considerations that have been discussed above, this wholesale acceptance of non-rational belief must be looked upon as normal. The mechanism by which it is affected demands some examination, since it cannot be denied that the facts conflict noticeably with popularly current views as to the part taken by reason in the formation of opinion.

"It is clear at the outset that these beliefs are invariably regarded by the holder as rational, and defended as such, while the position of one who holds contrary views is held

to be obviously unreasonable. The religious man accuses the
atheist of being shallow and irrational, and is met by a similar
reply; to the Conservative, the amazing thing about the Liberal
is his incapacity to see reason and accept the only possible
solution of public problems. Examination reveals the fact
that the differences are not due to the commission of the mere
mechanical fallacies of logic, since these are easily avoided, even
by the politician, and since there is no reason to suppose that
one party in such controversies is less logical than the other.
The difference is due rather to the fundamental assumption of
the antagonists being hostile, and these assumptions are derived
from herd suggestion; to the Liberal, certain basal conceptions
have acquired the quality of instinctive truth, have become
'a priori syntheses,' because of the accumulated suggestions
to which he has been exposed, and a similar explanation applies to the atheist, the Christian, and the Conservative. Each,
it is important to remember, finds in consequence the ra-
tionality of his position flawless, and is quite incapable of de-
tecting in it the fallacies which are obvious to his opponent,
to whom that particular series of assumptions has not been
rendered acceptable by herd suggestion." [1]

Human readiness to disregard the importance of facts,
even when significant issues are involved, is disclosed again
and again in political controversy. This is of special importance in discussing the function of the press, because
the newspaper deals to a large extent with what are perhaps not properly but are practically political matters.
Moreover, politicians represent greater educational achieve-
ment, though not perhaps greater native intelligence, on
the average, than the general public to which the daily
newspaper makes its principal appeal. The attitude of the
reading public toward the facts is no more competent than

[1] Reprinted from *Instincts of the Herd in Peace and War,* pp. 35–37, by W.
Trotter, by permission of The Macmillan Company, authorized publishers.

that of the senator, representative, or other purported student of public affairs.

The attitude of the politician is effectively represented in an incident of a recent Congress, retold by Walter Lippmann:

"At breakfast on the morning of September 29, 1919, some of the Senators read a news dispatch in the *Washington Post* about the landing of American marines on the Dalmatian coast. The newspaper said:

"FACTS NOW ESTABLISHED

" 'The following important facts appear already *established*. The orders to Rear Admiral Andrews commanding the American naval forces in the Adriatic, came from the British Admiralty via the War Council and Rear Admiral Knapps in London. The approval or disapproval of the American Navy Department was not asked. . . .

"WITHOUT DANIELS' KNOWLEDGE

" 'Mr. Daniels was admittedly placed in a peculiar position when cables reached here stating that the forces over which he is presumed to have exclusive control were carrying on what amounted to naval warfare without his knowledge. It was fully realized that the *British Admiralty might desire to issue orders to Rear Admiral Andrews* to act on behalf of Great Britain and her Allies, because the situation required sacrifice on the part of some nation if D'Annunzio's followers were to be held in check.

" 'It was further realized that *under the new league of nations plan foreigners would be in a position to direct American Naval forces in emergencies* with or without the consent of the American Navy Department. . . .' etc.   (Italics mine.)

"The first Senator to comment is Mr. Knox of Pennsylvania. Indignantly he demands investigation.   In Mr. Brandegee of

Connecticut, who spoke next, indignation has already stimulated credulity. Where Mr. Knox indignantly wishes to know if the report is true, Mr. Brandegee, a half a minute later, would like to know what would have happened if marines had been killed. Mr. Knox, interested in the question, forgets that he asked for an inquiry, and replies. If American marines had been killed, it would be war. The mood of the debate is still conditional. Debate proceeds. Mr. McCormick of Illinois reminds the Senate that the Wilson administration is prone to the waging of small unauthorized wars. He repeats Theodore Roosevelt's quip about 'waging peace.' Mr. Brandegee notes that the marines acted 'under orders of a Supreme Council sitting somewhere,' but he cannot recall who represents the United States on that body. The Supreme Council is unknown to the Constitution of the United States. Therefore Mr. New of Indiana submits a resolution calling for the facts.

"So far the Senators still recognize vaguely that they are discussing a rumor. Being lawyers they still remember some of the forms of evidence. But as red-blooded men they already experience all the indignation which is appropriate to the fact that American marines have been ordered into war by a foreign government and without the consent of Congress. Emotionally they want to believe it, because they are Republicans fighting the League of Nations. This arouses the Democratic leader, Mr. Hitchcock of Nebraska. He defends the Supreme Council; it was acting under the war powers. Peace has not yet been concluded because the Republicans are delaying it. Therefore the action was necessary and legal. Both sides now assume that the report is true, and the conclusions they draw are the conclusions of their partisanship. Yet this extraordinary assumption is in a debate over a resolution to investigate the truth of the assumption. It reveals how difficult it is, even for trained lawyers, to suspend response until the returns are in. The response is instantaneous. The fiction is taken for truth because the fiction is badly needed.

"A few days later an official report showed that the marines were not landed by order of the British Government or of the Supreme Council. They had not been fighting the Italians. They had been landed at the request of the Italian Government to protect Italians, and the American commander had been officially thanked by the Italian authorities. The marines were not at war with Italy. They had acted according to an established international practice which had nothing to do with the League of Nations.

"The scene of action was the Adriatic. The picture of that scene in the Senators' heads at Washington was furnished, in this case probably with intent to deceive, by a man who cared nothing about the Adriatic, but much about defeating the League. To this picture the Senate responded by a strengthening of its partisan differences over the League." [1]

It is largely the psychological situation that produces the differences of opinion, conscious and unconscious, concerning the quasi-public function of the newspaper. There are the political-minded, who would have the newspaper run in the interest of their particular political views. There are clergymen and others, who hold that the newspaper should be published with a view primarily to the maintenance of morality or some other abstraction—as held by them and not subjected to impartial examination. There are numerous other groups with similar points of view. These hold that the newspaper is primarily "a molder of public opinion," and this molding, according to their view, is not necessarily to be based on actual facts, investigated and proved true, but on assumed facts, uninvestigated, plus exhortation based on ethical, political, and other dogmas likewise not subjected to any critical examination.

[1] Reprinted from *Public Opinion*, pp. 17–20, by Walter Lippmann, by permission of Harcourt, Brace & Co., authorized publishers.

The Rev. David James Burrell, a prominent clergyman of New York, stated this point of view in a recent sermon, for the text of which he used the words: "As cold water to a thirsty soul, so is *good* news from a far country." (Italics mine.) In the course of his address Dr. Burrell said:

"We want a newspaper that shall publish the news. All the news? Well, hardly. . . .

"We want a newspaper that shall not merely reflect public opinion, but mold it, and mold it right. Nobody questions the power of the press. Dr. Talmadge made no overstatement when he defined an editor as 'a man who puts a thought on the end of a pen and hurls it to the uttermost parts of the earth.' But that statement is incomplete unless it be yoked up with John Foster's words, 'Power to the last atom is responsibility.' The bended bow of a ready writer may shoot either a message of relief or a poisoned arrow across the walls of a beleaguered city. . . .

"A Christian newspaper? Well, why not? If I throw a handful of iron filings into the air, they descend as harmlessly as thistledown, but, molded into a cannonball, they can sink a man-of-war. There are enough Christians in this community to demand and secure some sort of respect for their convictions; but never, never at the hands of writers who cavil at law and order and common morality, sitting under the cross and casting lots for the garments of our Savior.

"It is too much to expect of such men a rational presentation of the underlying forces that make for progress. To us the coming of Christ is 'the one supreme divine event to which the whole creation moves': to them it is nothing. If our Lord were to appear in the clouds of heaven today, what would the morning edition look like tomorrow? Where would the usual headlines be?" [1]

[1] *Marble Collegiate Pulpit*, Vol. 32, No. 13, pp. 2 and 8.

This position represents but a slight advance upon that of St. Ambrose in the fourth century: "To discuss the nature and position of the earth does not help us in our hope of the life to come. It is enough to know what Scripture states, 'That He hung up the earth upon nothing.' " [1] The advance made by the later writer is only in not categorically denying the significance of facts.

This view was in general that of newspapers themselves until very recently. In the early newspapers of this country and of other countries, the facts were invariably colored by opinion. Some lip service was given to the doctrine of objective facts, but it was always discounted by the practice of the paper and not infrequently by statements of the editor himself.

At the opposite extreme from the critics heretofore mentioned, stand those who would make the newspaper exclusively a disseminator of objective facts, even to the extent of omitting all editorial comment, all feature material, and everything else that is not strictly news. Few newspaper workers hold this ideal; they know, only too well, that the public demands features as well as significant facts, and they realize that a newspaper cannot be run without public support. Newspaper men generally, however, do hold, theoretically at least, the doctrine that the dissemination of objective facts is the primary if not the exclusive function of the press, and that all other possible functions should be subordinated to this.

This doctrine is based on the modern theory of popular government. Thomas Jefferson, as has been previously pointed out, observed that democracy worked best in rural districts. Temperamentally averse to cities, Jefferson held that the success of democracy in rural communities was due

---

[1] *Hexaëmeron*, I: 6, in Migne's *Patres Latini*, Vol. XIV.

to the superior qualities implanted in rural folk by the Creator. We know now that Jefferson's observation was right but his conclusion wrong. Democracy has ordinarily worked better in rural districts and in small communities because the individual voters are personally familiar with the local conditions and the local personalities. These matters are discussed in detail at town meetings, school district meetings, and other gatherings in which everybody has a voice. The people get the objective facts, then form their conclusions and record their votes, largely on the basis thereof.

As a greater proportion of the population has moved to cities, and as the problems of government have become more complex, the voters have been more and more unable to obtain, through personal observation or investigation, objective facts on which to base their voting, except on the local problems of small communities. Dependence for facts must be placed on the press. It is the only potentially satisfactory agency, existent or proposed, for this purpose. Successful popular government, being dependent on facts, is therefore dependent on the press. Moreover, all the other popular problems, not strictly governmental, have the same twofold dependence. Hence it is maintained, on grounds which can scarcely be successfully assailed, that the fundamental function of the newspaper is to disseminate the objective facts concerning matters of public concern.

While accepted as a practical reality by comparatively few, this ideal of the newspaper is gaining strength rapidly. Among the general public, it is an unconscious standard, but nevertheless a standard. The frequency of such remarks as "You cannot believe that newspaper article" and "That is only a newspaper story," bears witness to a public ideal that the newspaper should present the facts, even though it bears witness also to a common conviction that that ideal is being violated.

Additional Readings

Trotter, *Instincts of the Herd in Peace and War*, pp. 1–41.
Robinson, *The Mind in the Making*, pp. 14–48.
Edman, *Human Traits*, pp. 368–410.
Burrell, *Wanted: A Newspaper. The Marble Collegiate Pulpit,* Vol. 32, No. 31.
Lippmann, *Public Opinion*, pp. 1–32, 253–314.
Lippmann, *Liberty and the News.*

III

Public Charges Against the Newspaper

The public as a whole, as has been pointed out, has, consciously or unconsciously, a conception of the newspaper as primarily a disseminator of the objective facts of public significance. Whether this public would actually welcome the complete fulfilment of this function is beside the present problem and will be discussed later.

As is evident to every one, the public believes that the press is not fulfilling its function. Concretely, it charges the newspaper with not telling the truth; or, to put it more exactly, with not publishing the objective facts in an unbiased manner. Closer observers, both writers and speakers, accuse the newspaper of certain specific deficiencies in connection with its function of disseminating objective facts.

One of the fundamental charges is that the newspaper manufactures news. This charge is in general an example of the generally recognized fact that the public, when it sees things going badly in any part of the social system, attributes the difficulties to conditions which have disappeared. The manufacture of news was at one time a common practice. Ben Jonson in the *Staple of Newes* accused the journalists of the seventeenth century of barefaced faking. *The New York Sun's* reputation began with the famous Moon Hoax in 1835. This was a series of pure inventions by Richard Adams Locke purporting to contain important astronomical discoveries made by Sir John Herschel, the noted scientist. *The Sun* asserted that the fake "hurt nobody" while Edgar Allan Poe wrote: "From the epoch of the hoax the *Sun* shone with unmitigated splendor. Its success firmly established the 'penny system' throughout the country, and (through the *Sun*) consequently we are indebted to the genius of Mr. Locke for one of the most important steps ever yet taken in the pathway of human progress."

Not only was Locke not dropped from the paper when the hoax became known, but he was given further duties on the paper and later became editor of *The Brooklyn Eagle*. The historian of the paper, Frank M. O'Brien, writing as late as 1917, referred to the hoax as "magnificent." [1]

The word "roorback" was added to American language by a fake in 1844, in which a writer credited to a traveler named Roorback a description of the horrors of slavery, including the false statement that James K. Polk, then candidate for the Presidency, had branded forty-three slaves with his initials. Published in several up-state journals in New York, it was exposed by *The Albany Argus* and became a "roorback," reflecting on the integrity of Polk's opponents and helping to bring about his election.

A faked proclamation, purporting to be by Abraham Lincoln, was prepared in 1864 by two young newspaper men, who succeeded in getting it into two newspapers. The young men planned to use it for playing the stock market. The newspapers were temporarily suspended, but were allowed to reopen their offices when the government was convinced that they were not to blame.

A notorious example of faking, or near-faking, took place in the summer of 1899, when certain well-known insects,

[1] For details of the fake, see O'Brien's *The Story of the Sun,* pp. 64–102.

including most conspicuously the blood-sucking cone-noses, appeared in somewhat larger numbers than usual and bit a number of persons. Upon this flimsy foundation of fact the newspapers built up a superstructure of misleading stories of injury and death through bites of a so-called "kissing bug." Many of the injuries reported were due merely to bites of the mosquito or of the common horsefly. By means of conscienceless lying, the press of that day caused veritable terror in many American towns and cities, and undoubtedly produced much actual illness among the hysterical.[1]

More recently, when Harry K. Thaw was first committed to a hospital for the insane, interviews were faked between Thaw and other noted inmates of the asylum. Another faked story told how Thaw had been appointed superintendent of the chickens at the Matteawan hospital, and quoted rules purported to have been laid down by him for running a chicken farm. Numerous other stories about Thaw had no more foundation than these.

In very recent times supposedly humorous stories, to the careful, intelligent reader obviously fakes, were sent out, or supposedly sent out, from small towns in New York and New Jersey. Newspaper men asserted that these did not deceive the public and were too ridiculous to be accepted as fact. It is probable, however, that some persons did accept them as fact and that many others were prejudiced against the newspaper as an institution by reason of its offering this faked material.

---

[1] For discussion of the actual situation, in comparison with newspaper reports, see L. O. Howard, *The Insects to Which the Name "Kissing-bug" Became Applied in the Summer of 1899*, United States Department of Agriculture, Division of Entomology, Bulletin 22, New Series, pp. 24–30; also L. O. Howard, *Spider Bites and "Kissing Bugs," Popular Science Monthly* 56: 31–42.

In the latter years of the nineteenth century, as yellow journalism was developing, the practice began of definitely misrepresenting the news in the headlines. The news stories themselves were reasonably accurate, but over a story dealing with the slight injury of two or three persons in a fire would be printed a head asserting that many had been killed. The obvious purpose was street sales.

In this period, also, faking in connection with pictures was introduced. Pictures were in demand by the sensational press, and were harder to get than they are now. If a prominent personage died and the newspaper lacked a picture, it was not uncommon to get from the files a cut of a person who somewhat resembled the deceased personage and publish this as an actual portrait. In some cases drawings were made up from imagination and halftones from them were published as from actual photographs.

As late as 1903 Edwin L. Shuman, then literary editor of *The Chicago Record-Herald*, wrote in explanation of the current journalistic attitude toward facts:

"Newspapers frequently receive important pieces of news that lack the necessary details for presenting them with due dignity of length. It becomes necessary to supply the missing materials in the office. In many cases this can be done with the aid of the 'morgue' or cabinet of biographical and obituary materials that is maintained in every wide-awake newspaper office. Sometimes books of reference will supply much of the needed information. In not a few cases, however, it becomes the duty of the reporter or editor to supply the missing materials from his inner consciousness, drawing much upon his memory or his imagination. So long as he uses his imagination only upon non-essential details the method appears to be permissible.

"This kind of license has become absolutely necessary in writing the reports of events which will be past when the paper appears, but which must be described before they occur. Intense rivalry for the latest news long ago drove editors to the use of the 'journalistic imagination' in such cases. The amount of matter that is prepared in this way, especially for evening papers, probably would surprise the average reader. The fact will account for many of the inaccuracies of the press, but on the whole it is cause for wonder that the newspapers can be as accurate as they are under the circumstances. The ethics of the subject may be left to the individual reader. I merely record the fact that the practice exists to some degree on every enterprising paper." [1]

The practices heretofore mentioned are no longer those of any considerable number of newspapers. Where they now occur, they are likely to be sporadic, and usually the fault of a dishonest reporter or correspondent, who acts either wholly of his own violition or because of the expressed or implied direction of an editor—himself a subordinate— to get copy regardless of its character. Certain photographic services practice faking. A newspaper knowing this fact assumes risk, if not actual culpability, in buying any photographs from such unreliable sources.

There is, moreover, occasional use of a photograph, apparently by specific design, in such a way as to amount to manufacture of news, as when a sensational metropolitan daily published a picture of Mexican children, standing in water, as evidence that they had been driven to take refuge from bandits who had overrun the country. The same picture had been previously published as representing merely a group of bathing Mexican children. The newspaper which published the picture, it is worthy of note, was

[1] *Practical Journalism,* pp. 103–104.

endeavoring to persuade the United States to make war upon Mexico.

Regardless of the ethics of the matter, such practices on the part of newspapers are certain to alienate readers and convince them of the dishonesty of the press. *The New York World* tells how, when it published by mistake a picture of Newcastle-on-Tyne as one of Hartlepool, a reader wrote in, stating that he recognized the picture and adding the following paragraph:

"You can't fool ALL of the people ALL of the time, and when you do not happen to have on hand an illustration to accompany a news article, for goodness' sake don't try to hand us something near it. 'Just as good; they won't know any different,' is a policy which is inimical to the boasted fair-play attitude of your paper—and I have read it for a number of years."

In this case, the newspaper was fortunately able to convince its correspondent that the error was wholly unintentional.[1]

There of course still remains the temptation to the reporter to fake news, even when he knows his newspaper opposes it. The only safe principle to follow, as it is the only adequate statement of the situation, is: *There is no harmless fake.* The way in which faking of tremendous social harm develops from the so-called "harmless fake" is well told by Ralph Pulitzer, whose newspaper, *The New York World,* was a pioneer in steps looking toward accuracy and fair play:

"The philosophy of faking is worth your attention. The tendency to fake usually begins in some trivial story of a

---

[1] The incident is discussed in the *Biennial Report of The World's Bureau of Accuracy and Fair Play,* 1915, pp. 16–17.

broadly humorous character in which the writer embroiders a comical situation with additionally ludicrous exaggerations which make no pretense to being anything but imaginative. You cannot lay your finger on anything definitely wrong about this story, since it gives its facts faithfully enough and brands its fiction so frankly that no one can be deceived.

"The only thing wrong about it is that it is apt to be the first step to worse things. For the writer, congratulated on the brightness of this first story, will possibly, on the next occasion, write a story equally funny, equally frank in admitting to being partially the fabrication of a comic fancy, but a story in which the facts and the fiction blend so together that the reader cannot be sure where the one ends and the other begins. Such a story has crossed the line which divides the enjoyable from the reprehensible. But they say it 'does no one any harm' and is exceedingly droll, and a managing editor with a keen sense of humor is eager to get out a bright paper, and so in it goes.

"Now, the writer's next literary effort is apt to be one in which the humorous facts constitute the merest rudiments of the story, and the story itself as a work of comic fiction could stand unsupported, even if what few facts there were were removed. And still those responsible for that story being in the paper may all ask a critic what conceivable harm that story did any one. And at first you can't point to any one that it hurt. But a moment's thought will show you that while this story hurt no one that it was about, it did hurt several other persons and one institution. It injured the reporter who wrote it, the city editor to whom he reported it, the copy reader who edited it, the managing editor who printed it, and the newspaper which published it. It hurt these men by insidiously dulling the keen edge of their sense of accuracy, and it injured the paper by injuring them. For that particular reporter is now ripe to apply the same methods to writing a serious story about serious people and serious events, and instead of using his fancy for the broadening of humor we shall find him using his imagination for the heightening of tragedy, the deepening of pathos, the sharpening of the dramatic. And still on certain papers you will find the excuse that these stories 'do no one any harm.' And the men who make this excuse do not seem to realize that any harm has been done when the general public uses the term 'newspaper story'—which should be a synonym for facts —as a euphemism for a lie.

"The next step in this Fake's Progress is the descent from embroidering untruths on a background of serious facts to fabricating a serious story out of the whole cloth without a single fact to base it on, but using real persons for characters. About on a level with this last perpetration is the cynical 'stunt' which a very few papers encourage and a few have condoned where the reporter, if he cannot find that a good story has happened, actually hires people to make it happen, let us say to shoot up a saloon in a gang war that has grown lean of news, or to hang a prominent employer in effigy in some strike, as in the story I have already told you.

"The last step of our reporter, now grown hopelessly irresponsible, unscrupulous, and cynical, is a fake that bespatters some honest man's character, or besmirches some virtuous woman's reputation, which ruins spotless lives and has led innocent people to self-inflicted deaths. The reporter who has sunk to this depth of degradation might just as well be a murderer; in fact, there are a good many honest murderers whose boots he is unworthy to lick. But fortunately at this point the libel law, which might well have become effective considerably sooner, is very apt to take a hand in the game; and although our present criminal libel laws have been able to send all too few newspaper crooks to jail, yet heavy money damages are likely to visit a partial retribution on the offending paper, and when the pocket nerve, which is the nearest approach to a conscience which such a paper possesses, begins to ache, the reporter who lost this paper some of its money is apt to walk the plank. And there you have the whole progress, from the bright little flight of the imagination that was so laughable and harmless, down to the criminal piece of work that wrecked innocent lives, brought a rotten reporter to final ruin—and lost an unscrupulous paper a fraction of its ill-earned dividends.

"As the fake varies in viciousness, so the responsibility of the newspaper varies in degree. For some fakes which a paper prints, plausible stories sent in from distant correspondents whose accuracy it has no reason for doubting and no means of corroborating, it would be grossly unjust to blame that paper. All it can do in a case like this is promptly to discharge the guilty correspondent, but this it should do ruthlessly. Fortunately most of the fakes charged against the press belong to this class. For other fakes that get printed, neither newspapers nor reporters are responsible. These are the fabrications exploiting everything from rapid-transit systems down to chorus girls which the pernicious press agent is constantly plotting to worm into a newspaper. Experienced editors are generally equipped with a sixth sense for the detection of the press agent yarn, but, nevertheless, these wretched concoctions do quite frequently slip in, and the newspapers get the blame.

"Then there is the case where the newspaper innocently prints a fake by one of its reporters or correspondents and subsequently fails through good nature, weakness, or a blunted sense of accuracy to discharge the writer. Here the paper immediately assumes a large share of responsibility for the fake. It not only encourages that particular reporter to gain extra space rates by further faking of one-stick items into one-column stories, but it tempts other honest reporters to do likewise.

"The last case is where the paper itself deliberately stimulates faking in its writers or actually engineers a fake itself. This fortunately is exceedingly rare. There are papers which cynically avow their motto to be: 'Facts merely embarrass us!' But you can pretty well count all of them in this country on the fingers of your two hands. They may be enjoying the fleeting prosperity that even a monstrosity at a side show can enjoy, but they are evanescent. They are built on slime instead of on rock. Any institution that flourishes on an appeal to morbidness by the aid of mendacity can have but a precarious hold on prosperity or even on life itself.

"I am afraid that in the last few minutes I have drawn a dark picture, but fortunately it applies to few papers, and the number of these papers is growing smaller from year to year. I don't think any one who knows his newspaper history will question the fact that the striving for accuracy is steadily growing keener and more wide spread. Newspapers are spending more and more money and efforts in the verification of news. It has been estimated that a responsible paper, for every four dollars that it spends on originally getting a piece of news, spends *six dollars* on verifying it."[1]

The gradual disappearance of faking is due partly to the fact that news is now easier to obtain and to verify because of the increased organization of newspapers and press associations, partly to the growing realization of the value of news and the growing sense of the dignity and honor of their profession on the part of practicing newspaper men. In the case of less scrupulous journalists, the disapprobation and contempt manifested by the public toward fakes have had their influence.

The extensive faking in times past, however, has crystallized into a public belief that they still are the common methods followed by newspapers. Not only the general public, but experienced observers, believe that such practices are common. For example, Roland G. Usher, professor of history in Washington University, St. Louis, recently asserted: "The cable news you read is not written

[1] Pulitzer, *The Profession of Journalism: Accuracy in the News*, pp. 12–15. Reprinted by permission

on the other side except in rare instances. The cost of cabling such lengthy accounts would be prohibitive. That news is sent in dispatches of from eight to ten lines and is expanded by the re-write men into two columns of stuff." Professor Usher's charges were answered by Frederick Roy Martin, general manager of the Associated Press, who pointed out that in the cable dispatches "the only omission is a few small words like *the, and*, etc., where the meaning is perfectly plain and which in no way abbreviates the plain context of each sentence and line and of the dispatch as a whole." The daily cable report was given by Mr. Martin as containing about 10,000 words.[1]

C. V. Van Anda, managing editor of *The New York Times*, presented figures showing more than 9,000 words daily by cable and wireless from correspondents of his paper.

The long persistence of charges after the basis for them has largely or even wholly disappeared makes it of utmost importance for the newspaper to deal as fairly as possible with its public. Dishonesty or unfairness today will be quoted by publicists and by the general public twenty-five years hence.

None of the other charges which are generally made against the newspaper have been superseded so fully by changes in newspaper practice as has the charge of manufacturing news. There has been a gradual improvement in newspaper practice, although it is by no means sufficient to acquit the newspaper of charges made against it.

For example, while the complete manufacture of news has practically disappeared, the practice of putting "hokum" into the news still exists. "Hokum" is sure-fire stuff. Every nation has its own varieties, determined by the taste and interests of the mass of the population. The use of

[1] *The Editor and Publisher*, February 17, 1923.

"hokum" in the movies and in popular fiction has probably stimulated its employment in the newspapers.

"Hokum" in the United States is sentimental, mixed up with a certain vapory idealism and at the same time with a devotion to financial and business success. From the days of *The Log Cabin Boy Who Became President* to the days of Harold Bell Wright, the taste of the dominant middle-class public in "hokum" has only slightly wavered. That riches come to the righteous and God-fearing, that nevertheless there are other things, such as true love, which are superior to financial considerations, and that the great are invariably kind to dumb animals—these are a few of many bits of "hokum" which are firmly fixed in the middle-class mind.

Newspaper men know the public taste for "hokum" and they frequently add to news stories matter which they have invented in order to make the facts appear to conform to the public ideas. For example, not long ago a young woman, heiress to an estate of some millions of dollars left her by a relative, was married to her childhood sweetheart. The facts of the case were that the young woman and the young man had grown up in the same town. Her parents were not wealthy, even according to the standards of the place. His people, on the other hand, had considerable means, owning stores not only there, but in several other towns. His interests at the time of his marriage to her amounted to perhaps a quarter of a million dollars. He is a pleasant young business man, a member of the various local booster and social clubs. Upon their marriage they went to live in a country house owned by him, containing perhaps twenty rooms and situated in the midst of a considerable estate.

In the actual facts of the case there was little .which

could arouse the sentimental interest of a middle-class reader. Ingenious reporters developed a wholly different story. The young man was a poor boy but idealistic. It was discovered by the reporters that he had some slight talent in drawing and that some years before he had made a series of political cartoons for a small paper in his state and had done more or less other desultory work with his pen. This made him, according to the reporters' story, a struggling young artist who had given up the possibility of making a living by business in order to follow his art. Moreover, when he found that his beloved had become heir to millions he was represented as having been unwilling to ask her to marry him, but she, magnanimous in the possession of a fortune and in the knowledge that love for her was mingled with idealistic devotion to art, brought it about that they were married. Thereupon they went to live in a little cottage by the river, the same twenty-room home heretofore mentioned. Thus the public was again given touching evidence that dollars cannot stay the progress of true love and that love and art will live happily together in the meanest hovel.

A more sinister use of "hokum," approaching the out-and-out fake, is reported by Isaac D. White of *The New York World:*

"In a factory town in a neighboring state a young woman was drowned one evening while out boating with one of the mill hands. The latter, drenched to the skin and badly frightened, was the first to give word of the tragedy. He explained that while changing seats the boat had been upset accidentally about one hundred yards from shore, and that after trying vainly in the darkness to reach the woman, he, being a poor swimmer, with difficulty managed to save himself. The boat and oars were found adrift in the lake next morning, and later the body of the girl was dragged from the bottom near the spot pointed out by her companion. There were no marks or bruises on the body, and the cause of death was shown to be drowning.

"The unfortunate victim of what was so clearly an accident was a prostitute, in personal appearance most unprepossessing. She had a harelip, was tongue-tied, and had been half-witted from her birth. She was the boon companion of the most notorious woman in the town. Every New York newspaper had hurried men to the scene, and the facts connected with the drowning and the young woman's reputation were promptly made known to the reporters by the local police. And yet readers of one New York newspaper were led to believe that 'a beautiful young society girl' had been drowned while 'defending her honor'; that the entire community was aroused and indignant over the failure of the authorities to arrest her companion; that some unknown and mysterious influence was protecting him in open defiance of law and justice. The community was indignant, right enough, but the indignation was directed toward the reporter who had deliberately lied about the town and its officials. This faker continued to send out lying reports from the town for a week, and then capped the climax of his faking by inducing an ignorant relative of the dead girl to sign a petition to the Governor of the State denouncing the local authorities and praying His Excellency to interfere to the end that justice might be done. The reporter published the petition in his paper before mailing it to the Governor." [1]

Another type of "hokum," more common because it can be practiced with less ability, consists merely in attaching to persons who appear in the news certain stereotyped titles to make them more interesting to the reading public. A man who chances to be arrested while in evening clothes, may be referred to as "a popular clubman" or as "a prom-

[1] White, *Fairness and Accuracy in Journalism, The New York World,* December 22, 1912.

inent man about town." A woman accused of immorality is not uncommonly spoken of as "pretty" or "beautiful" regardless of her actual appearance.

The tolerant but cynical attitude often taken by newspaper men toward this form of misrepresentation is illustrated in the humorous story published in 1917 in *The Chicago Herald*, in which the "Old Reporter" offers some questions for examining aspirants for reporters' licenses. Some of the questions asked were these:

"How many high-balls does it take to turn a prominent club-man into a well-known figure in the city's night-life?

"How many pink teas does it take to turn a social leader into a queen of the exclusive set?

"How does a scion differ from a rich man's son?

"How much must a father leave before his daughter may be called an heiress, and how long after forty-two may she still be young and beautiful?

"Write a sentence with the words 'It is alleged' in such a manner that the reader will have no doubt the allegation is true.

"Describe the wedding romance of a wealthy and prominent teamster and a beautiful young heiress of Goose Island.

"On what page must the story of a fire be printed so that it may be spoken of as a conflagration?

"How long after a woman is arrested for shoplifting does she become a former actress?

"Would you refer to the deceased parents of a deceased politician as having been poor but honest, or would you not better call them immigrants who came to the land of golden promise to make their way in the New World across the sea?

"What do you know about campus beauties? Are they also pulchritudinous co-eds or only rah-rah girls?" [1]

[1] Quoted by *The Literary Digest*, Vol. 54, pp. 1021–1022.

It is argued by reporters who engage in the practice of manufacturing "hokum" that in most cases it is harmful to nobody. The story of the young married couple pleased a vast circle of readers and confirmed them in their sentimental views of life. It presumably amused the persons concerning whom it was written and possibly pleased them, because it placed them before the world in a semi-heroic light, and being heroic is distasteful to very few. The story is simply fiction "founded on fact," as stories in our childhood days used to be headed.

But what of the people who had lived in the town and region where this couple had lived since childhood? What was the effect of the story upon them? Precisely the same effect that is produced by every such story. It added further evidence to their conviction that nothing published in a newspaper can be depended upon. Persons who know of this and similar circumstances will view with the same suspicion a truthful story dealing with international relations or any other subject of vast public importance.

To a considerable extent the belief also prevails that where news exists it is falsified, or misrepresented, with or without design on the part of newspapers, before it reaches the public. Any unprejudiced observer finds evidence of falsification in such a matter as the handling of the news during and after the Russian Revolution. When a newspaper itself publishes cartoons satirizing the news stories relating to the "death," "imprisonment," and other vicissitudes that did not happen to Premier Lenin, there can be no room for doubt as to the extent of falsification of the Russian situation. Again, the quotations made by Messrs. Lippmann and Merz in *A Test of the News* show a considerable amount of absolute falsification. Headlines announced the "smashing" of the Bolshevist army, the burning of Petrograd, and, later, the capture of Petrograd by Yudenitch's army! [1]

Falsification of the news is, however, much less common than the average reader probably believes. At the present time, no matter recorded with a reasonable degree of certainty is likely to be falsified. No newspaper would think for a moment of falsifying the result of an election, the quotations on the stock exchange, or the verdict of a jury, even if it were not in competition with other newspapers which would furnish the facts to the public. Falsification occurs most often where the actual facts are difficult to obtain and rumor and belief are accepted in their stead.[2] The simpler and more honest plan, of course, would be to publish no news when there is none that the editors consider dependable. This plan newspapers refuse to adopt, maintaining that competition compels them to print a certain amount of news about any given event or supposed event. They salve their consciences and attempt to pro-

[1] *A Test of the News*, pp. 30 and 33. This study, published as a supplement to *The New Republic* of August 4, 1920, analyzes all news about Russia in *The New York Times*, chosen as an outstanding newspaper, from March, 1917, to March, 1920.

[2] Mr. Lippmann seems to the writer to go too far, however, in his discussion of the relation between the certainty of news and the system of record (*Public Opinion*, pp. 342–345). He lays insufficient stress on the possibility of carelessness, laziness, or some less common psychological trait in the reporter or copyreader. For example, in reporting the famous speech of Senator La Follette on September 20, 1917, the Associated Press inserted the word "no" in such a way that a sentence reading, "We had grievances," was altered to "We had no grievances." The error was apparently unintentional on the part of the editor who prepared the story, and was ascribed by the Associated Press in its apology to lack of care. The writer, however, would raise the question whether it is not one of those errors which modern psychology has shown to be determined by the unconscious of the individual making them. The editor, opposed to Mr. La Follette, might unconsciously insert in a story matter which would naturally produce an unfavorable impression of the speaker. More attention might wisely be given to problems of this character in the study of journalism.

tect themselves against complaining readers by the use of such expressions as "it is rumored," "it is believed," "high officials assert," which are held by the courts, certainly not in advance of public conscience, to be no defense in suits for libel. If the publication of rumors, even labeled as such, can harm the individual to such an extent that he can recover damages the same as if they were stated as facts, their publication, even when not libelling any individual, must certainly be held by enlightened public opinion to be subversive of that clear view of human affairs which the press should give and upon which the citizen should act.

Another common charge against the newspaper is that the news is often suppressed. In the average small town it is not a difficult matter to persuade an editor to suppress a piece of news that may be distasteful to an advertiser or, more commonly, simply a friend and subscriber. In the larger towns and cities such suppression is less common.[1] Certain newspapers, too, suppress news that is unfavorable to views that the paper holds. For example, when several hundred thousand dollars was subscribed by members of the New York trade unions for support of the steel strike at a meeting to which New York papers gave front-page position, Pittsburgh newspapers omitted all reference to the subscriptions or the meeting.[2]

The problem of news suppression is complicated by the fact that no newspaper of considerable size can print nearly all the copy that comes to it. There must be a

[1] The example of this most often quoted—which, however, occurred a number of years ago—is that of the Philadelphia newspapers which unanimously suppressed the story of the suicide of a prominent Philadelphia advertiser in New York when caught in disgraceful circumstances. (See Ross.) *The Suppression of Important News*, in Bleyer's *The Profession of Journalism*, p. 84, and Sinclair, *The Brass Check*, p. 227.)

[2] Interchurch World Movement, Commission of Inquiry, *Public Opinion and the Steel Strike*, pp. 150–151.

process of selection. Some news must be suppressed. What critics of newspapers mean when they assert that news is suppressed by the papers is, of course, that news of public significance is suppressed. The matter is in part a question of judgment, but unfortunately unjudicial bias often creeps in. The newspaper desirous of retaining the respect of its constituency for itself and for newspapers generally, will be sedulous to avoid suppressing news which it might be assumed would be to its interest to suppress.

Again, it is charged against the newspapers that news is colored by the policy of the paper. Examples of this are quoted from headlines and from news stories themselves. The coloring of news, where it takes place, is ordinarily in the interest of the policy of the paper or what reporters and editors on the paper conceive to be its policy, although there is some coloring by reporters because of personal prejudice, due not infrequently to the attitude of persons in the news toward reporters. Numerous examples of the coloring of news may be found in any industrial controversy on the part of papers representing both sides. The coloring of news on the part of the conservative press is aired more frequently because conservative papers are in the majority. Examination of radical newspapers, however, will show a similar amount of coloring in behalf of their side of any controversy. For example, the Federated Press, which professes to "report objectively," ends a news story concerning a critic of Upton Sinclair thus:

"There is no special reason apart from orders higher up why Carter should rush to the defense of the colleges, since, according to his own story, he never went beyond the district school." [1]

[1] *The Federated Press Bulletin*, Vol. 5, No. 9, p. 4.

There is likewise much coloring of the news in the interest of sensationalism, partly as a policy of newspapers, partly by reporters of their own volition. Discussing a recent divorce suit, Edwin W. Booth, editor of *The Grand Rapids Press,* published in the place where the case was tried, said of the treatment of this case in certain Chicago and Detroit newspapers: "If a verbatim report of the trial had been given to the public the public might have fairly judged of the merits of the case, but, following the rule, the charges against Trotter were played up and his defense played down. Though adjudged innocent by the court, at the bar of public opinion Trotter's reputation was so damaged th.. I personally question whether his work will ever be the same, not only in this city, but in other cities where the unfair news was carried." [1]

The coloring of news by means of headlines is the subject of well justified criticism. Many persons doubtless read only the headlines or get from the headlines an attitude toward the news which even an unbiased story following the head will not erase. The practice of expressing opinion in heads is increasing, to the distinct lowering of the value of the press as a disseminator of objective facts. Following, for example, are eleven heads used over the same letter written by President Harding to Stephen E. Connor, secretary of the Federated Shop Crafts of the Central Railroad of New Jersey:

HARDING REBUKES ROADS THAT FAIL TO SETTLE STRIKE—STUBBORN MINORITY IS DECLARED RESPONSIBLE FOR COAL SHORTAGE AND FREIGHT CONGESTION.

—*New York World.*

[1] *Addresses and Proceedings of the Fourth Annual Meeting of the University Press Club of Michigan,* p. 101.

HARDING BLAMES RAIL STRIKERS FOR SUF-
FERING—WRITES JERSEY CENTRAL SHOP LEAD-
ERS HE REGRETS REFUSAL OF MINORITY OF
MEN TO RETURN TO THEIR JOBS—FEARS WORSE
CONDITIONS—CRITICIZES THEM FOR HOLDING
UP COAL DELIVERIES AND DEMORALIZING IN-
DUSTRY.

—New York Tribune.

HARDING DEMANDS END OF RAIL STRIKE—HIS
LETTER ON SHOP CRAFTS TROUBLE STIRS NEW
JERSEY CENTRAL—HE HELPS RELIEF FUND—
HOLDS MINORITY OF INTERESTS RESPONSIBLE
FOR FAILURE TO SETTLE—RAILWAY ENTERS
DENIAL—ASSERTS POLICY HAS BEEN IN ACCORD
WITH PRESIDENT'S PROCLAMATION.

—New York Herald.

RAIL SHOPMEN ARE REBUKED BY PRESIDENT
—NO REASON FOR STRIKE OF LAST YEAR TO
DRAG LONGER, MR. HARDING DECLARES.

—Buffalo Express.

SHOP STRIKE UNJUSTIFIED—HARDING SAYS—
MINORITY BLAMED FOR TRAFFIC CONDITIONS.

—Cincinnati Enquirer.

HARDING EAGER FOR END OF R. R. SHOPMEN
STRIKE—SEES NO REASON FOR MEN HOLDING
OUT.

—Chicago Tribune.

BARRING OF SHOPMEN SCORED BY HARDING—
PRESIDENT BLAMES UNCOMPROMISING RAIL-
ROADS IN PART FOR SHORTAGE OF COAL—HE
SEES NO JUSTIFICATION—IN LETTER TO NEW

JERSEY UNION LEADER HE SAYS MINORITY ROADS SHOULD FOLLOW LEADS OF BIG LINES.
—New York Times.

HARDING ADVISES SHOPMEN TO YIELD—SEES NO REASON FOR FURTHER DELAY IN REACHING FULL SETTLEMENT—WRITES UNION OFFICIAL.
—Philadelphia Public Ledger.

HARDING ASSAILS RAILROAD STRIKE—PRESIDENT SEES NO REASON FOR FAILURE OF MINORITY TO EFFECT PEACE—BLAMED FOR CONGESTION—INTERRUPTED COAL DELIVERIES, TOO, ASCRIBED TO FAILURE TO END WALKOUT.
—Baltimore Sun.

HARDING RAPS STRIKERS—PRESIDENT TELLS RAIL SHOPMEN ALL SHOULD BE BACK AT WORK —BLAMES THOSE WORKERS OUT FOR INTERRUPTION OF COAL DELIVERIES.
—Chicago Daily News.

HARDING ASKS ALL SHOPMEN TO END STRIKE —PRESIDENT SEES NO REASONS FOR PROMULGATING OF RAIL UNION WAR.
—Rochester Democrat-Chronicle.

It will be observed that of these eleven newspapers several assert that the president blames certain railroads for failing to settle the strike and others that he blames the strikers for continuing the difficulty. Still others show a certain degree of prejudice in one direction or the other. Only two, *The Cincinnati Enquirer* and *The Baltimore Sun,* treat this news in a strictly objective manner. It is a significant fact, as showing the attitude of interested parties toward the unbiased handling of news, that the clip sheet of the American Federation of Labor, known as the *International Labor News Service,* spoke disparagingly of the head in *The Cincinnati Enquirer,* which it characterized as "meaning nothing at all," and that in *The Baltimore Sun,* which, it asserted, "is as meaningless as *The Cincinnati Enquirer.*"

Less significant, so far as direct effect upon public life is concerned, but much more widely noticed, is the inaccuracy which marks the columns of American newspapers. Every reader of newspapers knows of instances in which errors have been made to his knowledge. He knows that his friend's name or his own has been misspelled. He has seen an item in his daily newspaper referring to a "Stratibury" violin or has seen *The Mind in the Making* and *The Americanization of Edward Bok* referred to as "popular works of fiction." Or he has seen Edna St. Vincent Millay referred to as "Edna Stevincent Hillay" in a newspaper popularly reputed to be one of the best edited in America.

In one newspaper of the writer's acquaintance the following head appeared on the first page: SENATE REJECTS YAP TREATY BY 50 TO 23 VOTES.[1]   The lead of the story follows:

"Washington, Feb. 28.—Dividing virtually on party lines, the senate refused to amend the Yap treaty today in the first test of strength on any case affecting the international covenants negotiated at the arms conference.   Vote was 50 to 23."

In this case the incompetence or laziness of the copyreader was such as no reporter, however ignorant, could have excelled.

In point not only of accuracy but of the other desiderata

[1] *The Leavenworth Times,* March 1, 1922.

in which the press is subject to criticism, it is evident to any unprejudiced student that the newspaper does better than would the average intelligent observer of events. Any one who has heard testimony by unbiased and careful witnesses as to the most readily observable matters has inevitably been struck by the disparities among the various stories. Likewise, everyday conversation makes it obvious that the average individual regularly alters facts to suit his opinions. He may indulge in this consciously or unconsciously.

On the other hand, this is not an argument sufficient to justify the present practices of the press, although it is often presented as such. It only introduces mitigating circumstances. As an argument in itself, it has little more value than the insistence of a barber that he is competent because he can cut hair better than the average citizen who has never worked at the barber's trade. The newspaper is supposed to be written by persons trained and experienced in fulfilling the function of the press. In his professional capacity, a journalist is to be compared not with the general public but with the best journalists elsewhere.

Additional Readings

Lippmann, *Public Opinion,* pp. 338–357.

Macy, *Journalism,* in *Civilization in the United States,* pp. 35–51.

Ross, *The Suppression of Important News,* in Bleyer's *The Profession of Journalism,* pp. 79–96.

Sinclair, *The Brass Check,* pp. 228–313.

Lee and Sinclair, Discussion of *The Brass Check.* *The New York Globe and Commercial Advertiser,* June and July, 1921.

Holt, *Commercialism and Journalism,* pp. 1–49.

Sullivan, *National Floodmarks,* pp. 160–166.

Interchurch World Movement, Commission of Inquiry, *Public Opinion and the Steel Strike,* pp. 87–162.

Salmon, *The Newspaper and the Historian,* pp. 138–157, 412–467.

Gladden, *Tainted Journalism, Good and Bad,* in Thorpe's *The Coming Newspaper,* pp. 27–50.

Lippmann and Merz, *A Test of the News,* Supplement to *The New Republic,* August 4, 1920.

IV

DEFICIENCIES OF THE PRESS: THE MATERIALISTIC INDICTMENT

Almost every one who makes charges against the press has an explanation for the deficiencies of which he complains. The explanations commonly given and generally believed are in line with certain tendencies of the popular mind, manifest in its attitude in all subjects of public concern.

To begin with, there is in the popular mind what may be termed "an atrocity habit." Every trouble that arises appears to be result of an atrocity perpetrated on democratic government, on morality, on civilization, or on something else that intensely matters. Or, perhaps, the trouble itself seems to be the atrocity. Closely associated with this is the conspiracy habit of mind, a feeling that some group of persons is constantly plotting the ruin of what is to the best interests of the public. Atrocity, conspiracy—these two ideas stir the public from lethargy.

This is no new phenomenon in American history. The Boston Tea Party was the result of an atrocity complex. For a number of years the Anti-Masonic Party existed on the basis of atrocity and conspiracy complexes, and these became so powerful that in Vermont, according to historians, every Masonic lodge surrendered its charter. In the Civil War, an atrocity complex was dominant in the North and a conspiracy complex in the South. Every

64

Southerner was a brutal slave-driver, while every Northerner was a scheming Yankee enrolled in a conspiracy to destroy the resources of every state below Mason and Dixon's line. The Populist Party throve on the atrocities of the older parties. One of its principal apologists urged the necessity of raising "less corn and more hell." The Progressive Party owed its rise and also its downfall largely to the two habits of mind. It was the idea of busting the trusts and imprisoning their officers that roused the crowd. Complexes feed on themselves, and when the Progressive leaders ran out of dragons to exhibit before execution the people sought other atrocities and conspiracies and other men to denounce them.

With the appetite of the American citizen so whetted for atrocities and conspiracies, it is no wonder that he was fed on them during the recent war, by superpatriots on the one hand and by radicals—when the administration gave them a chance—on the other. It still continues. The Communist Party, the I. W. W., the Socialists, union labor, and scores of other bodies are asserted to be in a conspiracy to commit atrocities against "Americanism." From the standpoint of the radicals, there is a capitalistic conspiracy, definitely organized and heavily supported, to suppress every suggestion of change in the *status quo*.

The public attitude toward the newspaper, expressed in general conversation and in printed books and articles, accepts the atrocity and conspiracy theories. Not infrequently the suggestion is made that the propietors of a given newspaper ought to be arrested. The typical article on the subject proposes a law of some sort to govern the press. The explanations commonly given for the deficiencies of the press are in accord with this point of view.

One of the reasons often presented for the failure of

newspapers to present the news accurately and fairly is that sensational handling of the news builds circulation. It is true that certain newspapers have built up their circulations while pursuing a sensational policy and have used this policy as a circulation argument. In some cases they may have adopted a sensational policy as a means of getting circulation. The most conspicuous examples of ultra-sensational journalism, the Hearst newspapers, have generally followed the practice of building their circulations among groups of the population that were not previously reading any newspapers. Getting newspaper circulation is always expensive, but this is the cheapest way to get it. It is easier to persuade a person not taking any paper to take one—particularly if you offer him a green glass butter dish or a picture of Daniel among the lions—than to persuade some one already taking a paper to stop that one and take yours. In the latter case a good deal of time-consuming and consequently expensive argument must be added to the butter dish or the picture. The people who were not newspaper readers when the Hearst organization made its big campaigns belonged to the relatively unintelligent. An interesting divorce case loomed larger to them than a serious international problem. They could understand divorce where they could not understand international relations. The newspaper that appealed to them had to be sensational. There is still a question, however, whether the newspaper became sensational in order to appeal to them or the newspaper, being sensational to begin with, made a natural appeal.

As to American newspapers in general, the theory that they become sensational in order to attract readers is not tenable. A study of circulation figures, as given by the Audit Bureau of Circulations, shows that in the average

city which contains one or more "yellow" newspapers, one
or more conservative (in handling of news, not in political
theory), and one or more that lie between the two, the
biggest circulation is held by a moderate paper, a "yellow"
paper stands second, while conservative papers trail along
toward the end.

On any newspaper of size, however, circulation is merely
a means to an end, that end being advertising. As already
stated, a large newspaper seldom gets enough from subscribers and newsstand buyers to pay its paper bills. An
extremely large circulation means a quantity circulation;
that is, a circulation which appeals to the advertiser mainly
on the ground of its size. A small circulation, if among the
rich or well-to-do, is a quality circulation. Rates for
advertising are invariably compared on the basis of the
amount charged per agate line or per inch for each unit
of circulation. The rate on a quantity circulation is always
very low. On a quality circulation it is very high. The
minimum rate ranges on daily newspapers in large cities
from $1.08 per milline (quantity papers) to $7.31 per
milline (quality papers).[1] It follows that a newspaper may
be very profitable financially on an exceedingly small circulation.

Another reason given by many for the deficiencies of the
press is that the support of newspapers may be purchased
for cold cash and thus enlisted in the support of certain
corporations, politicians, or even criminals. When a newspaper is supporting what appears directly contrary to the
public welfare, it is often surmised that its support has been
bought as a business transaction.

That cases of direct bribery have taken place, there is

[1] The milline rate is the rate per agate line per 1,000,000 of circulation.
For data on specific papers, see the *Standard Rate and Data Service.*

no doubt. Fremont Older, in *My Own Story*,[1] gives details of such transactions. The writer personally knew one publisher—fortunately, for the welfare of journalism, now dead—whose support, he is convinced, could be bought for any measure. Though this publisher had the only newspaper in his city, a franchise which he had vigorously supported, making use of numerous dishonest tactics, was defeated five to one. Every member of his own staff voted against the franchise. This was the culmination of long years of attempted betrayal of the public trust. So thoroughly did the public finally become aroused that the publisher sold his paper and left the city. Old newspapermen will all recall reporters who accepted bribes personally.

Direct bribery of newspapers or newspapermen is now, the writer is convinced, extremely rare; it is doubtful if it ever was common. It has disappeared along with direct bribery of public officials and individual voters. The public, though apathetic and long-suffering, at last revolted against bribery of all sorts. With the public vigilant and strongly opposed to bribery, those who would corrupt officials, the electorate, or the press, have found that even where takers of bribes can be found, the expected results cannot be delivered.

Those who do not hold that newspapers are bribed directly, often maintain that they are bribed indirectly by the promise to give or the threat to withhold advertising. Like direct bribery, this practice is less common than it once was. It has always been attempted by advertisers more often than it has succeeded. Some years ago, when bicycles were becoming popular, all the bicycle advertising was withdrawn from one of the New York dailies because it pointed out that bicycles were being sold at from five to

[1] Pp. 23–30.

six times their manufacturing cost. Again, the department stores of the same city withdrew their advertising from a newspaper because of its attitude on the tariff, and even stopped the credit accounts of customers who took the newspaper's side in the controversy.[1] More recently, as mentioned earlier in this work, *The Boston Evening Transcript* lost a great quantity of shoe advertising because it printed the actual news about the shoe industry in Massachusetts. In each of the cases mentioned, the advertisers eventually came back to the newspapers.

Numerous instances might be given of newspapers that have acceded to the requests of advertisers to suppress this or that. In every such case, of course, the demands of the advertisers steadily increased. Requests for suppression or publication of certain statements come to every newspaper from advertisers—and from non-advertisers—who in most instances probably do not realize the dishonorable and anti-social character of their requests.

Large papers, on the whole, are not so much affected by promises or threats on the part of advertisers as are smaller papers. It is regarded as poor business to let the advertiser gain the impression that he controls the papers. In any case, as has been often shown, he cannot stay out of a good advertising medium for long. There is, however, a tendency, even on large papers, to show a kind of gratitude to (or at least consideration for) the advertiser by accommodating him (usually without his request) in news matters which affect him. Such is commonly the impelling motive when newspapers omit the names of department stores in which accidents, cases of shoplifting, and other unpleasant incidents take place. Gratitude for advertis-

---

[1] The two incidents, with numerous others, are treated in Holt's *Commercialism and Journalism*, pp. 66–68.

ing is obviously a ridiculous motive on the part of a strong newspaper. The sale of advertising is purely a business transaction, in which the advertiser expects to receive a profitable return from the space which he has purchased. Any disposition of gratitude to the advertiser is a relic of days when newspaper circulations were small, advertising rates were wholly unstandardized, and advertising was inserted largely as a charity to the publisher. It behooves no publication today to put advertising on a charity basis.

In the case of newspapers that have not strong financial backing, the temptation to please advertisers is strong. The average newspaper obtains only 35 per cent of its revenue from circulation, and this proportion is much smaller in the metropolitan daily. Slight as it is, circulation revenue fluctuates greatly. Except in the case of small country weeklies on which subscriptions are paid by the year, the reader is under no obligation to continue the paper from week to week or even from day to day. Every issue must sell itself to the reader's interest. In addition to the fact that they furnish the bulk of the revenue of a newspaper, advertisers tend to be more constant in their patronage than do readers.

That the financial problem is a real one is well known to any one familiar with the publishing business. An investigation made ten years ago in Kansas showed that 82 per cent of the newspaper plants in that state were operating under mortgages.[1] Dr. Talcott Williams, who is probably as well-informed as any other man about metropolitan journalism, states that there are few if any American dailies which have not gone on the "red" in the past fifty years, so far as their yearly profit and loss account is concerned.[2]

[1] Thorpe, *The Coming Newspaper*, p. 13.
[2] *The Newspaperman*, p. 146.

As a business, publishing a newspaper is precarious.

The extent of influence of the advertiser upon the news in the press cannot be definitely stated. Doubtless it is much less than is commonly supposed. One realistic factor, commonly overlooked, which influences strongly against special favors to advertisers is the fact that advertisers are competitors. What pleases one may displease a score of others, and vice versa. Moreover, in the mass of news the advertiser has little if any personal interest. While undoubtedly it has its influence, advertising cannot be considered a principal reason for the deficiencies of the press.

This does not mean, of course, that the influence of advertising in this direction is to be disregarded as of no significance. Every effort should be made to put advertising on a strictly commercial basis. The stronger newspapers are resorting to various means of accomplishing this. One well-known newspaper which endeavors to maintain its standards of fact in the news and its definite policies in the editorial columns even when they are unpopular, for years has carried a heavy reserve investment in a distant part of the country in order to be assured of sufficient funds in case the attitude of the paper results in financial loss. Financial independence, it cannot be too strongly urged, is likely to be necessary to ethical independence in the case of any institution which derives its revenue from private sources but owes responsibility to the public.

Again, as explanation of the deficiencies of the press, it is stated that newspapers are strongly influenced by business connections, such as ownership by capitalists or interlocking directorates between the newspaper and a railway or other public service corporation, a great farming enterprise, or a land speculation scheme. As a matter of fact, not many newspapers have such connections. When the connections do exist, there is evidence of their effect. Of similar character is the effort of bankers to influence the policy of weak newspapers by granting or withholding loans. Personal ambitions of a publisher, in politics, social life, or business, may likewise lead the newspaper astray.

The explanations that have been presented represent the causes commonly assigned for the deficiencies of the American newspapers, for their failure to maintain a higher standard of objective fact. The explanations involve both the atrocity and the conspiracy. They represent an essentially materialistic view of the press. Embodying all of them is a prevalent feeling that the newspaper has become essentially a prostitute, and after the manner of prostitutes has allied herself with other sinister interests. Many persons express agreement with Upton Sinclair when he says:

"What is the Brass Check? The Brass Check is found in your pay-envelope every week—you who write and print and distribute our newspapers and magazines. The Brass Check is the price of your shame—you who take the fair body of truth and sell it in the market-place, who betray the virgin hopes of mankind into the loathsome brothel of Big Business. And down in the counting-room below sits the 'madame' who profits by your shame; unless, perchance, she is off at Palm Beach or Newport, flaunting her jewels and her feathers." [1]

It is natural that this point of view should be widely accepted. As has been stated, some evidence can be found in support of it. It is simple. It agrees with the atrocity and conspiracy habits of mind which are so widespread.

If, however, this were an adequate explanation, one would expect to find in the radical press, which is bitterly opposed to capitalism, the accuracy, fairness, and absence of bias

[1] *The Brass Check*, p. 436.

which it is alleged are thwarted in the rest of the newspapers by capitalistic conspiracy. Instead, one finds in the radical press substantially the same deficiencies as in the conservative press. The deficiencies of the press are explained to no considerable extent by any materialistic theory.

Additional Readings

Sinclair, *The Brass Check*, pp. 32–38, 221–249, 258–310.
Holt, *Commercialism and Journalism*.
Belloc, *The Free Press*.
Williams, *The Newspaperman*, pp. 145–151.
Older, *My Own Story*.
Adams, *Success*.
Adams, *The Clarion*.
Thorpe, *The Coming Newspaper*, pp. 1–26.
Angell, *The Press and the Organisation of Society*, pp. 11–75.
Anderson, *The Blue Pencil*. *The New Republic*, December 14, 1918, pp. 192–194.

V

DEFICIENCIES OF THE PRESS: A REALISTIC EXPLANATION

The materialistic view of the newspaper heretofore presented, is, as has been pointed out, in relatively small part true. The principal causes for the failure of the American newspaper to fulfill its primary function are not those which are commonly alleged, but are to be found much more deeply imbedded in American life. They are subtle, slow-working, and intertwined with many other characteristics of our civilization.

Not corruption, but ignorance, inertia, and fear—the same type of ignorance, the same type of inertia, and the same type of fear that permeate American life—are the fundamental causes for the failure of American newspapers in giving the public the facts which the public has a right to demand.

Persons who come to this country from Europe, familiar with the better of the newspapers there, are astonished at the ignorance displayed by American reporters and copy-readers about the simplest matters, though their astonishment is always tempered when they discover the same sort of ignorance among high school and college students. Common geographical and historical facts, the names of well-known persons, to say nothing of economic, political, and artistic terms, are ludicrously twisted by reporters, and the copy-readers often enough pass the errors by.

Such ignorance, though lamentable, would not present so serious a face were it not for the fact that the average reporter does not seek enlightenment. He is afflicted with inertia, such as keeps a voter from seeking to understand political issues or even from voting at all. Given an assignment on an unfamiliar subject, the reporter will start out cocksure without consulting a reference book or even a more intelligent member of the staff of his paper. He will return and write his story without even looking into a dictionary. The story is currently told of a city reporter, sent out to interview John Burroughs, whom he fatuously supposed to be the inventor of the adding machine. After some minutes of conversation with the naturalist, the reporter began to feel some doubt as to the mechanical knowledge of the man he was interviewing, and blurted out:

"You'll pardon me, Mr. Burroughs, but what line of business are you in?"

A reporter of the writer's acquaintance on a widely quoted daily, who had finally got sufficiently perplexed over a religious story to turn to the despised reference book, attempted to look up the name of Mary Magdalene in *Who's Who in America*.

Circumstances of this sort make the American newspaper undependable in its reports of technical matters and to a less but still considerable extent in its ordinary news. In most cases the errors made do not directly affect the public judgment on significant issues. They are, however, a distinct discredit to American journalism.

On the other hand, when a reporter is placed on an important international story, he can do much damage by ignorance. Not a little of the misrepresentation of European conditions during and after the war was due to ignorance of history, geography, and economics on the part of American correspondents. The Warsaw correspondent who conveyed the impression that Vilna is historically Polish was, in all probability, simply ignorant and too lazy to ascertain the facts. The same excuse would hold for American editors who printed his story without verification.

In economic affairs, the ignorance of the typical American newspaper man is most marked. Here, again, he merely reflects the ignorance of the American public; indeed, he is less ignorant than the vast majority of his readers. Members of the British Labour Party and of the French trade unions have a familiarity with economic history and current economic problems such as shames the American college graduate. The various directions in which economic change has been brought about in Europe, in Australia, in other parts of the world, the very terms which are in common use in modern economics, are unknown to, or misunderstood by, the average journalist in this country. It is not surprising that he stamps as "bolshevistic," "radical," "socialistic," or "anarchistic"—he uses all these and many other terms with fine disregard of their meaning—all plans for altering the *status quo,* or that he utterly confuses the news relating to such plans.

Quite as serious is the ignorance of the American reporter concerning what constitutes evidence. Evidence is not an easy matter to deal with practically; the experience of the courts is sufficient proof of this fact. Nevertheless, there are some fundamental principles that the reporter should, but frequently does not, recognize. For example, it is a well understood principle that nothing should be accepted as fact on the uncorroborated statement of a single individual. So important is this that even in scientific investigation, where men of special training and presumably impersonal zeal for the truth are engaged, it is a common practice for individual records to be kept by two persons. Yet reporters—and perhaps news editors even more readily —accept as fact or something very close to fact what is at best uncorroborated testimony of one person and at worst mere rumor.

The acceptance as fact of statements by persons high in official life, in the United States or in other countries, or by persons who claim, without actually possessing, some special knowledge of a subject, is especially common among reporters. This is in part mere credulity on the reporter's part. In part, however, it represents inertia. There is no easier way to get news than to obtain it from some single individual. Again, there is no easier way to handle such news than to accept it as fact without examining its intrinsic probability, the actual qualifications of the individual giving it to speak with authority on the subject, or the freedom of this individual from official or personal bias which may lead him, intentionally or unconsciously, to misrepresent the facts.

The misinterpretation of the Russian situation from the time of the Revolution on was due to a considerable extent to the credulity and ignorance of American reporters. While it is true that the actual conditions in Russia during this confused period are far from clear now, it is at the same time evident that the news furnished by American correspondents, especially during the counter-revolutionary campaigns, was notoriously unreliable. The comment made by Messrs. Lippmann and Merz on the credulity of reporters in this severe test is illuminating:

"The analysis shows how seriously misled was *The Times* by its reliance upon the official purveyors of information. It indicates that statements of fact emanating from governments

and the circles around governments as well as from the leaders of political movements cannot be taken as judgments of fact
by an independent press.   They indicate opinion, they are
controlled by special purpose, and they are not trustworthy
news.   If, for example, the Russian Minister of War says that
the armies of Russia were never stronger, that cannot be accepted by a newspaper as news that the armies of Russia *are*
stronger than ever.   The only news in the statement is that
the Minister *says* they are stronger.   By any high journalistic
standard, the Minister's statement, if it deals with a matter
of vital importance, is a challenge to independent investigation.

"The analysis shows that even more misleading than the
official statement purporting to be a statement of fact, is the
semi-official and semi-authoritative but anonymous statement.
Such news is fathered by such phrases as:

" 'Officials of the State Department'

" 'government and diplomatic sources'

" 'reports reaching here'

" 'it is stated on high authority that'

"Behind those phrases may be anybody, a minor bureaucrat,
a dinner table conversation, hotel lobby gossip, a chance acquaintance, a paid agent.   Dispatches of this type put the
editor at home and the reader at the mercy of opinion that
he cannot check, and it is time to demand that the correspondent take the trouble to identify his informants sufficiently
to supply the reader with some means of estimating the character of the report.   He need not name the individual source
but he can 'place' him. . . .

"The analysis indicates also that even so rich and commanding a newspaper as *The Times* does not take seriously enough
the equipment of the correspondent.   For extraordinarily
difficult posts in extraordinary times, something more than
routine correspondents are required.   Reporting is one of the
most difficult profesions, requiring much expert knowledge
and serious education.   The old contention that properly
trained men lack the "news sense" will not stand against the

fact that improperly trained men have seriously misled a whole nation. It is habit rather than preference which makes readers accept news from correspondents whose usefulness is about that of an astrologer or an alchemist. Important as it is for the press to read lessons in efficiency to workingmen, employees, and politicians, it is no less important for the press to study those lessons itself. Measured by its responsibility and pretensions, the efficiency of the newspapers is not what determined men could make it." [1]

When the ignorance of the American journalist, and specifically the American reporter, is mentioned, the argument is often advanced that greater knowledge is impossible. The error of this conclusion may readily be seen if one will compare the articles about Russia published in 1920 in the better dailies of the United States with those of Mr. Arthur Ransome, published in *The Manchester Guardian*. Knowledge of general conditions and readiness to investigate with meticulous care in order to get specific data are manifest in the work of this English reporter. For examples, Mr. Ransome's articles stated such pertinent facts as these: The proportion of manufactured goods imported into Russia prior to the Revolution; the exact number of available locomotives in the country each year from 1914 on; the number of horses mobilized in Perm Government for timber production; the monthly output of coal per man in each of a number of coal mines; the proportion of the nominal working hours kept in the state metal-working factories; the precise membership of the Communist party; the details of organization that secured for this party, with its small membership, actual dominance. These data, with numerous others, are brought together in such a way as to give a clear picture of economic conditions. While much

---

[1] *A Test of the News*, pp. 41–42.

of Mr. Ransome's information is not news, in the sense of dealing exclusively with immediately contemporaneous happenings, it comprises those objective facts which are so closely related to events as to make the latter unintelligible without a knowledge of the former.[1]

To take an example nearer home, American newspapers frequently sensationalize, ridicule, or ignorantly misrepresent scientific conventions.   In 1922, however, *The New York Times* sent to cover the annual meeting of the American Association for the Advancement of Science Alva Johnston, who was fitted by temperament and training to handle the facts of science.   Dealing with an enormous variety of scientific subject matter, Mr. Johnston, by reason of his prior knowledge and his care as to the exact facts, produced daily during the convention a group of news stories which for accuracy, clearness, and interest could hardly be surpassed.   The award of the Pulitzer prize to these stories as the best example of a reporter's work during the year is evidence of a growing concern for newspaper writing of indubitable reliability.[2]

The instances cited show clearly that sufficient mental equipment and energy in seeking facts are by no means unattainable on the part of the reporter.   Ignorance and inertia exist on newspapers simply because knowledge is not demanded.   "A good story" is the most common expression in many a newspaper office.   The exact truthfulness of the story is too seldom called into question.   There is a prevalent feeling in newspaper offices that the public demands "good stories" and is not concerned much with their accuracy.   Well-written stories, based partly on facts,

[1] Much of Mr. Ransome's material is reprinted in his book, *The Crisis in Russia*, which will be especially useful where files of *The Guardian* are inaccessible.

[2] The articles appear in *The New York Times*, December 28 to 30, 1922.

semi-humorous leads written in by copy-readers, and flores-
cent, artificial heads (developed, it is true, as an exigency
of newspaper makeup), make such a combination as may
well drive considerations of clear-cut knowledge completely
out of the reckoning. Real knowledge of modern economics
is less likely to gain promotion for a reporter on the
average paper than the ability to write an interesting but
largely untruthful story about a street fight over the ownership of a custard pie. The public, the editor says, is more
interested in the humor of custard pies than in economics.

Closely related to ignorance and inertia, but even more
powerful in its influence against complete and impartial
truth-telling by newspapers, is fear. Fear is a characteristic
not simply of newspapers; it is a characteristic of the
American people. It is not a physical fear; Americans have
shown courage and endurance times without number. It is
rather an intellectual and spiritual fear, based on nothing
tangible, on nothing which affords a reasonable basis for
fear. It takes most conspicuously the form of fear of
and deference to the herd, the whole body of people within
the nation. Necessary for preservation of the race in some
distant period of its history, it remains today as an anomaly.

It is to be admitted at once that because of man's gre-
garious nature there is everywhere a natural desire—slowly
diminishing, however—on the part of the individual to identify himself with the herd with respect to his conviction and
opinions. While he may not desire, or may even actively
shrink from, the approbation of the great mass of people,
he will nevertheless seek the approval of a small body, "a
herd within a herd," with which he conforms in matters of
opinion.[1] On the other hand, there is an excessive defer-

---

[1] For a detailed discussion of this phenomenon, see Trotter, *Instincts of
the Herd in Peace and War*, pp. 23–41.

ence to and fear of the herd, which prevent intellectual and, to a considerable extent, other progress. This attitude has long been recognized as one of the dangers of democratic government. In his treatise *On Liberty*,[1] John Stuart Mill pointed out that if either of two opinions "has a better claim than the other not merely to be tolerated but to be encouraged and countenanced, it is the one which happens at the particular time and place to be in a minority." Going on with his discussion, Mill stated that tyranny of established ideas tends to "a dead uniformity of taste and opinion and method of life that will finally lead to a more than Chinese stagnation." In the United States, the development of excessive deference to the herd is due not only to the natural tendency of democracy but also to the fact that in early times the unity of the nation, such as it was, was based on common antipathies more than on common sympathies.

So far as fear is concerned, it is obviously useless. As Dr. Freud says, "everything that happens would be consummated just as well and better without the development of fear."[2] The general recognition of the uselessness of fear probably accounts in part for the fact that it masks or rationalizes itself in other guises. No individual is willing to admit, even to himself, that he is a coward. The fear complex is inhibited by the psychic censor, and manifests itself in indirect and devious ways. Conduct actually inspired by fear is explained by the individual on the basis of various false rationalizations.

Hence, fear, though carrying none of the moral stigma which attaches to corruption, is much more devastating. Corruption presents a clear-cut issue of right and wrong, of honesty and dishonesty. There is always the chance that

[1] Chapter II.
[2] *A General Introduction to Psychoanalysis*, p. 341.

the crook will see this issue and determine to try to follow the right.   Fear involves no clear-cut issue of any sort.   Unadmitted as a motive by the person who is actuated by it, fear undermines every intellectual, ethical, and emotional resistance.

Fear in journalism begins with the reporter and permeates every part of the newspaper organization up to the publisher. Conversation with many reporters has convinced the writer that the vast majority are fundamentally honest.   It likewise has convinced him that the vast majority are either liberals or radicals, though in many cases unintelligent ones.   If, however, one picks up the average newspaper today and reads the stories written by these men, one will find a certain bias toward conservative and reactionary policies and against liberal and radical policies.   Presumably, if these men unconsciously varied from strict objective truth in writing their stories, they would vary in the direction of their own convictions; namely, in a liberal or a radical direction.   What is the explanation of their varying in exactly the opposite direction?

The average critic of the newspaper, unfamiliar with newspaper practices, attributes this to instructions issued by the publisher to his staff that matter must be written with a certain bias.   In some cases, such orders are issued—practically always, however, by publishers who are in no sense professional journalists but are rather business men running newspapers as they would run factories.   On most papers run even by men of this type, there are no such orders. Most instruction sheets issued to the members of newspaper staffs urge the importance of accuracy and fairness.[1]

A new managing editor comes to a newspaper.   He calls the members of the staff together and says to them:

[1] See examples of such sheets in Appendix A, pp. 211–238.

"Boys, the thing I want you to do is to get the news. We want all the news and we want it accurately. We don't care what it's about or whom it hits. There are going to be no sacred cows on this paper so long as I'm managing editor. If I see a sacred calf coming on, I'm going to choke it before it grows up."

The boys listen, then they go out smiling to themselves, and write the same old stories with the same old bias. What is the trouble?

Fundamentally, it is fear on the part of the reporter and employees immediately above the reporter. All, or nearly all, the newspapers that the reporter has seen, including the one on which he is working, have exhibited a conservative bias in handling the news. He believes that the publisher wants only stories with a conservative bias and that if he writes an important political or economic story showing no bias or showing radical or liberal bias, the story will not be printed and he may be fired. If nothing more, he feels that the story will be so altered by the copy desk as to maintain the conservative bias. The statements of the managing editor have not removed his fears. That functionary is considered by the reporter to have been "letting off steam," "trying to kid himself," or "just making a speech." The reporter is perhaps encouraged in his beliefs by the city editor and the copy-readers—men who have grown old and cynical in the newspaper office and who could not readily find employment outside of it. There is instilled into the young newspaper man's mind the feeling that the publisher is involved in various capitalistic enterprises, that his business and social associates are all capitalists, and that he is publishing the newspaper in the interests of capitalism.

Thus is formed a hapless circle. Because of what newspapers he has read and because of what older newspaper men have told him, the young newspaper reporter gives a bias to what he writes. Other reporters, coming after him, will have read what he has written, will perchance listen to his talk, and will follow his example.

The same reasoning applies to such an organization as the Associated Press. As has heretofore been intimated, critics such as Mr. Upton Sinclair [1] hold that the Associated Press is essentially corrupt, maintained in the interests of capital. The situation rather is like this: Except where a special bureau is maintained, the Associated Press paper in each town—practically always a politically conservative paper—is, by virtue of its membership, the Associated Press correspondent for that town. The actual handling of the correspondence is, as a rule, turned over to some bright young man on the paper. This bright young man knows that there are other bright young men on his paper who would be glad of the job. Consequently, he is not going to do anything to cause a chance of his losing the position. He follows the beaten path of conservative bias in writing the news which he sends to the Associated Press. Quite beside the mark is the possibility that material written in a wholly definite way might be acceptable. The point is that the reporter disbelieves this, it may be for excellent reasons, and is actuated by the fear of losing his job.

The morale of the reporter may be further broken down by such circumstances as the fact that occasionally a "yellow" newspaper may keep a man to engage in dishonorable activities, such as picture-stealing, browbeating of witnesses, and even bribery. A man of this type is usually a

[1] *The Brass Check,* pp. 353–376.

partial invalid, a drunkard, a dope fiend, or a man weak-
ened by some other form of dissipation.   Reporters see the
activities of a man of this sort and, knowing that he can be
relied upon to do anything he is asked to do, think it not
worth while to fight hard for such ideals of journalistic
ethics as intellectually they may retain.

The natural result of such situations is to produce in the
reporter the cynical attitude that a newspaper is a purely
commercial enterprise, and that it does not pay to try to be
honest upon it.   The newspaper comes to occupy, in his
estimation, the same position as a store selling groceries or
dry goods.   It sells what the people want, or what the
proprietor thinks the people want, or what, for some other
reason, the proprietor is determined to sell.   There is developed in the reporter the psychological phenomenon
known as dissociation of consciousness.   In one compart-
ment of his mind he keeps his convictions about truth-telling and his liberal or radical ideas.   In another compart-
ment he keeps the commercial principles which he is convinced are those of the journalistic world.   His attitude is
the same as that of the deacon who cheats his customers on
weekdays on the conviction that business is business.
Neither the reporter nor the deacon is necessarily a conscious hypocrite.

The responsibility for this statement must not be laid
wholly upon the reporter.   The belief of the reporter that
his paper demands biased news may not be based on any
instructions from the publisher.   When, however, in the
face of such belief, the publisher remains silent or speaks
half-heartedly, the public concludes that the fear on the
part of the reporter is justified.   A publisher can make
it clear that unbiased reporting is the only acceptable reporting on his paper.   He can, if necessary, discharge all

editors and copy-readers who persist in conveying the opposite impression.

In most cases, the publisher does not face the issue at all. For one thing, in the large city he is more than likely not to be a professional journalist, but rather a business man, who has come up through the advertising department and who calls himself a "newspaper maker" rather than a newspaper man, an editor, or a journalist. He sees the newspaper as a business enterprise; intended to interest and please the public sufficiently to build a circulation which will bring in advertising. If he were asked categorically, he would say he wanted his paper to be honest, and he would mean it. He turns the editorial side of the paper over to competent men, to whom he gives few instructions. He assumes that they will run the paper satisfactorily, and so long as they do so he sees no reason for interfering with them. He reads his paper every day, and it seems to him a good, honest paper. His friends tell him it is a good, honest paper. The utter dishonesty of misrepresenting the news by means of giving it a specific bias has never been a concern of his.

In case the paper is corporately owned and managed by a board of directors, the truthfulness of the news becomes a matter of still less concern. A group of this character is always more cautious, less ready to interfere so long as things seem to be going fairly well, than any individual in the group.

The consolidation of papers under single ownership, individual or corporate, is likely to lead to equally unfortunate results.

The publisher or publishers, moreover, are subject to intellectual and spiritual fear—fear of the herd and deference to the herd. This is a factor more potent than any fear of the publisher on the part of the employees of the newspaper. Fear of the herd permeates newspaper workers from the publisher to the youngest cub reporter.

The newspaper, as at present constituted, is essentially a herd institution; and the herd in the United States constitutes much more clearly a mass formation than in any other great country. It is held together by a definiteness of faith unequaled except in a supposedly infallible Church. A long list of taboos—sexual, political, economic, and social —are dogmas of the American faith. Like the dogmas of an infallible Church, the dogmas of American faith are subject to no critical examination. The person who holds them may be able to give no more satisfactory reason for his belief than the believer in justification by faith or justification by works. Yet questioning of the dogmas convinces their holder that if you are not a heretic you are at least a vulgar fellow. Even those who profess willingness to test their beliefs usually approach them with a favorable prepossession, and merely attempt—unconsciously, it is true —to find logical ground for continuing to hold the doctrines. There is no genuine self-doubting.

Obviously devotion to the truth, for its own sake or as the sole guide to conduct, is not encouraged by a dogmatic system. Indeed, the people of the United States are notorious for their ostrichlike attitude toward all truths which will not climb up on their shoulders and purr. A motion picture censorship board recently barred from a widely known film the words, "It's a boy," and substituted "The boy is better," thus protecting American modesty against the unfortunate truth that children are born. Like the little girl in her attitude toward the boys, the American people do not like truths; they like "nice" truths.

The herd dogmas constituting the American deposit of

faith are ingrained in newspaper folk, from the proprietors down. The sympathy with the mass of people demanded by the contemporary newspaper with the emphasis on "human interest" often brings with it the masses' view of life. Devotion to absolute truth being in nowise encouraged by the dogmatic system, the tendency, in the absence of any set policy whatsoever, is to exclude from the papers anything, however true, which violently conflicts with herd dogmas.

For many years news of women and women's organizations was treated flippantly by newspapers, the serious facts of the subject being excluded or misrepresented. This is no longer the case. Some have ascribed the change to the fact that women not only have the vote but also determine what paper the family shall take. This is a shallow explanation. The real reason for the change is that the herd attitude toward women has changed, a general conviction having developed to the effect that women are people, and newspaper men have changed—in large measure unconsciously—with the herd.

The news concerning Russia, so far as it was not influenced, as previously pointed out, by ignorance and lack of understanding of the ordinary canons of evidence, was colored not through actual corruption of the press but because of the feeling of the press that the herd tradition was against Soviet Russia. And so it was. It is true that the herd tradition in this direction was directed in large measure by the newspapers, but they in turn had accepted propaganda from official and semi-official sources. This propaganda was skillfully prepared so as to bring the doctrines of Soviet Russia into apparent conflict with such American beliefs as the outward sanctity of marriage, democratic government, and private ownership of property.

Again to quote from the study by Messrs. Lippmann and Merz:

"The news as a whole is dominated by the hopes of the men who composed the news organization. They began as passionate partisans in a great war in which their own country's future was at stake. Until the armistice they were interested in defeating Germany. They hoped until they could hope no longer that Russia would fight. When they saw she could not fight, they worked for intervention as part of the war against Germany. When the war with Germany was over, the intervention still existed. They found reasons then for continuing the intervention. The German Peril as the reason for intervention ceased with the armistice; the Red Peril almost immediately afterwards supplanted it. The Red Peril in turn gave place to rejoicing over the hopes of the White Generals. When these hopes died, the Red Peril reappeared. In the large, the news about Russia is a case of seeing not what was, but what men wished to see.

"This deduction is more important, in the opinion of the authors, than any other. The chief censor and the chief propagandist were hope and fear in the minds of reporters and editors. They wanted to win the war; they wanted to ward off bolshevism. These subjective obstacles to the free pursuit of facts account for the tame submission of enterprising men to the objective censorship and propaganda under which they did their work. For subjective reasons they accepted and believed most of what they were told by the State Department, the so-called Russian Embassy in Washington, the Russian Information Bureau in New York, the Russian Committee in Paris, and the agents and adherents of the old régime all over Europe. For the same reason they endured the attention of officials at crucial points like Helsingfors, Omsk, Vladivostok, Stockholm, Copenhagen, London, and Paris. For the same reason they accepted reports of governmentally controlled news services abroad, and of correspondents who were unduly intimate with the various secret services and with members of the old Russian nobility." [1]

In incidents such as these, newspapermen in part are themselves influenced to believe what the herd believes, because they are essentially of the herd, while in part they consciously publish through fear what they believe the herd wants—as they say, they "give the public what it wants."

In addition to the common herd instincts of the people of the United States, there exist the specific herd instincts of the several economic classes. The rich, the middle class, the proletariat, or laboring class, have each distinctive herd instincts. By inheritance, tradition, education, and associations, newspaper men and women usually belong to the middle class, which is fundamentally a trading class and hence interested chiefly in commercial affairs. The owner of a newspaper, even in the few instances in which he is a rich man, is likely to hold the standards, instincts, and ideals of the middle class.

There are few more striking phenomena in the United States than the contempt of any class for the class or classes below it and the snobbish regard of any class for the class or classes above it. Nowhere, moreover, are these qualities more manifest than in the middle class. With the attitude of the middle class what it is, the newspaper man —publisher and reporter alike—is annoyed if he is called a "bolshevik" or a "radical," even in a joking way. He may assert that he believes in radical doctrines, but in his unconscious mind there still exists the desire to stand among the sober members of his class, who never deny or thwart its herd instincts.

Moreover, in the rare instances in which he has got rid of

[1] *Test of the News*, p. 3.

his unconscious deference to his class and the class above him, he has a certain fear of them. They are articulate. The proletariat has herd instincts, just the same, but it is largely inarticulate. The newspaper need have no fear of it. And the ideal of truth is no part of the herd instincts of any class, rich, middle, or poor, any more than it is a part of the herd instincts of the people as a whole.

The smaller the community, the more pronounced is deference to the herd. The large city, by reason of its very size and lack of curiosity, affords protection to him who differs from the herd. The vast majority of the newspapers of the United States are published in small towns, and these newspapers are more carefully read and are more influential with their readers than are the city dailies. At the same time, they display less independence of the herd.

A single example will make this clear. It is a common practice of small newspapers to omit the names of persons arrested for ordinary crimes and misdemeanors, although in a small community these undeniably constitute news. The reason regularly given for omission of these names is that publication of them would cause sorrow to the innocent relatives of the offenders. It is obvious that this is a false rationalization, produced according to well-known psychological laws, to account for what is really the product of fear of the herd.

The fear of the herd is in part an unconscious phenomenon. This invisible censor is not only invisible to the average newspaper man; its very existence is unknown to him. If told that he is governed largely by deference to the herd, he would deny it. He would give a variety of excuses for what he does, chief among them that he is governed by his best judgment.

Now and then, when a paper does publish facts which

tend to conflict with herd dogmas, the herd—or part of it —manifests its shock of horror and resentment. It is not uncommon for subscribers to cancel their subscriptions or for advertisers to withdraw their advertising because a newspaper has published matter, usually undeniable facts, which they dislike. Those who do not break off their financial connections with the paper are prone to write letters of denunciation. In these latter days mobs of self-styled patriots have demanded of newspapers that the facts be misrepresented in the interest of private propaganda. In the smaller cities and towns, individuals and organizations bring pressure to bear to have printed as news, matter which at its best is editorial comment and at its worst plain misrepresentation of facts. In all these cases, naturally, pressure comes from the articulate sections of the community. Such incidents lend weight to the contention, often advanced by cynical newspaper men, that the American public prefers always a pleasant lie to an unpleasant truth. And one may venture the further conclusion that the cold objectivity of the truth is of itself unpleasant to those who have grown accustomed to warm, cozy lies.

Nevertheless, although essentially part of the herd, maintaining a herd institution, and showing constant fear of and deference to herd instincts, many a newspaper publisher of today considers himself essentially superior to the herd. In some cases he speaks as if he were divinely appointed a molder of public opinion and a leader of the herd. At the same time, he has a conscious distrust and physical fear of the herd, quite different from his unconscious intellectual and spiritual fear of and deference to the herd.

His distrust and fear of the people manifest themselves in conscious unwillingness to give the people the facts.

Such unwillingness is, of course, no new thing. Governmental opposition to newspapers in ages long past was due to governmental opposition to giving the people the facts—particularly the facts concerning government. In England it was at one time permissible to publish only foreign news, this being regarded as relatively safe for the people to read. When the regulations were relaxed and news of England could be published in English papers, concealment of the facts from the people was aided, partly by statutory enactment, partly by the judicial ruling that the greater the truth, the greater was the libel. This fine piece of judicial casuistry was justified on the ground that the truth is more likely to provoke disturbance of the peace than is falsehood. In those days, the opposition to publication of facts came from kings, from landed aristocracies, from wealthy merchant groups—minorities conscious of present power but fearful of their future ability to maintain themselves in the face of the numerical majority. Newspaper publishers stood out, even in the face of prison sentences, for the right to publish the facts.

There can be seen a certain justification for the attitude of the rulers of those times. They did not profess to believe in popular government; nobody, except a few inconsequential fanatics, professed to believe in it. The government was not a government of the people, nor did it intend to be. Why should the people have any concern with it?

Today newspapermen seriously maintain their right to withhold facts from the people, and have thus taken the place of those monarchs and lords and rich traders whom they vanquished generations ago. Yet the newspaperman who would withhold facts from the people lacks the justification which those old-time rulers had. He professes to believe in popular government. He is fond of referring to the Declaration of Independence, the Constitution, and the principles of democracy. At the same time, he is ready to withhold from the people the facts—and facts are the only basis on which the people can form sound, dependable judgments.

This development has been produced by a combination of factors. Important among these has been the increasing tacit acceptance, in American political, civic, and commercial life, of the doctrine that the end justifies the means— no new doctrine, but one which would have been frowned upon by the sturdier democrats of the early days of the Republic. There has also been an expansion of that specious motto, "Our country, . . . may she ever be in the right; but, right or wrong, our country," until it has reached the depths of absurdity, easily apparent in the addresses of "boosters," as "Right or wrong, our town" and even "Right or wrong, our club."

To the growth of such sentiments newspapers have lent their aid. Every one knows how news of serious disease in a town is often suppressed or "played down" lest the reputation of the place—created by the local Chamber of Commerce—as "the healthiest city within five hundred miles in any direction" should be shattered. People still remember the attitude of California newspapers toward the earthquake and fire in San Francisco. Many other examples might be mentioned.

The growth of the tendency to conceal the facts because of distrust of the people was immeasurably assisted during the World War. Beginning with the suppression of the facts in the possession of the administration in the autumn of 1916 in order to make effectual the specious plea that the President "kept us out of war," the practice was followed throughout the war of giving to the public only such facts as it was believed would aid in winning the war or in bringing credit to American diplomacy. The so-called "voluntary censorship," on the one hand, and the Espionage Act, on the other, showed plainly the governmental attitude toward giving the facts to the public. No one doubts the desirability of keeping wartime secrets from reaching the enemy, but it is exceedingly questionable whether anything is added to the morale of a democracy by concealing all facts which are not optimistic in their import. Certainly such a practice means immeasurable harm to the future intellectual integrity of that democracy.

This was an exceedingly favorable time to fix upon the newspapers the practice of concealing the facts. In war practically every newspaper, in deference to the herd if for no other reason, wants to appear completely patriotic and a supporter of the government in its every activity. With the administration committed to the policy of presenting to the people only such facts as it held the people should know, the newspapers not unnaturally followed the same practice —a practice, however, in which to a less extent many of them had, it must be remembered, been previously engaged. The practice became a more or less honored tradition in many newspaper offices, and with the passing of the war it has continued. The question is asked, time after time, "Is it safe to give the people all these facts?" The young reporter, ignorant and inexperienced, asks the question of himself before he writes a story. It is noteworthy, moreover, that the facts which are omitted are not commonly details of crime and vice, interest in which might be criticized as morbid, but facts of political, economic, and social significance.

In the United States there is no phenomenon more threatening to popular government than the unwillingness of newspapers to give the facts to their readers. No more serious indictment can be presented against any public or quasi-public institution than that it ever questions the wisdom of giving the people the facts. It may be asserted that the people are unintelligent, swayed by prejudice and unreason, and that they should be supplied with only such facts as will cause them to think and act wisely; i. e., in the way in which a given newspaper—or even editor or reporter—considers it wise for them to think and act. But what is making them unintelligent if not the newspaper which adopts such a policy? And who shall say that the people, possessed of all the facts, will prove less capable of judgment than the staff of the average American newspaper? The only other argument advanced in favor of this practice is even less worthy of serious consideration. It is that certain newspapers will suppress some facts and other newspapers other facts and that thus the people will get all the facts. As if a reader could legitimately be expected to go through a process comparable to the examination of witnesses in court, in order to discover the facts about public affairs!

The only chance for actual popular government is for all the available facts to be given to the people clearly and objectively. The people may not always be wise, but they can gain no wisdom save through experience. Any person —or any institution—which seeks to keep from the public any facts of public concern shows thereby that he has at heart no belief in popular government. If he professes such belief, he is either consciously a deceiver or irretrievably self-deceived.

Additional Readings

Ransome, *The Crisis in Russia.*

Press releases and other copy furnished by Science Service.

Articles on the convention of the American Association for the Advancement of Science. *The New York Times,* December 28–30, 1922.

Trotter, *Instincts of the Herd in Peace and War,* pp. 23–41.

Freud, *A General Introduction to Psychoanalysis,* pp. 340–355.

Mill, *On Liberty.*

Salmon, *The Newspaper and the Historian,* pp. 114–137, 195–248.

Hackett, *The Invisible Censor,* pp. 1–10.

Lippmann and Merz, *A Test of the News,* Supplement to *The New Republic, August* 4, 1920.

Ghent, *False Testers of the News. The Review* 4: 488–489, 509–511.

Hapgood, *Journalism,* in *Every-day Ethics,* pp. 1–15.

Bliven, *Newspaper Morals. The New Republic* 35: 17–19.

VI

The Principle of Objectivity Applied: Balance and Proportion

In the foregoing chapters, it may be pointed out, there has been laid down a somewhat elaborate philosophy of journalism, a philosophy which presents objectivity in the dissemination of facts as the primary ideal of the press. Now, granted that every one theoretically agrees with this philosophy and would like, moreover, to see it carried out in actual practice, how is this to be accomplished? Are there not certain practical applications to be made which involve at times most difficult adjustments?

It must be admitted at once that the practical application of this philosophy—as indeed of any philosophy—does involve difficulties. The press is a human institution, and no human institution ever conforms precisely to a consistent ethical or philosophical theory. That newspapers generally are moving gradually toward the goal that has been presented, however, there can be little doubt. Nor can it be doubted that still more rapid progress would be made were the ideal of objectivity more tenaciously and realistically held by journalists. The advance made in the natural sciences since they abandoned the chiefly speculative and adopted the investigative method is evidence of what may be accomplished in a human institution even against the most implacable opposition.

Among the definite problems which must be met and settled by the press—not once for all, but time after time in the work of a single day—is that of proportion and balance. This problem involves what is commonly referred to by the layman as "the suppression of news." It involves also to a considerable extent the problem of sensationalism, a charge frequently brought against the press by persons interested primarily in preserving certain ethical standards in life.

In the small town the problem of proportion and balance does not cut a large figure. The newspaper has ample space for covering the news of its community. Where a piece of news remains unpublished, the suppression may be assumed to be deliberate—an attempt on the part of the publisher to conceal facts from his readers. Likewise, there is little question as to the news value of any specific local event. The problem remains relatively simple.

This is not true of a larger paper, and the larger the paper, the more perplexing becomes the problem. Reporters on metropolitan dailies turn in many times as much copy as could be printed in the space available. In addition, a great deal more copy could be obtained through more detailed investigation. Obviously there is a large quantity of material of some news value that does not get into the papers. A great deal of news must be "suppressed"—simply in the sense of being omitted from the newspapers. This, of course, is not the sense in which the term is commonly used by critics of the press. When they say that news is "suppressed," they imply that matter of public importance is concealed for unworthy reasons.

A difficult problem thus comes before the editors of any large newspaper for solution. Not only does the suppression of news for unworthy reasons exist in actual practice, but it is generally supposed to exist to a larger extent

than is really the case.   Moreover, there must be considered
the real importance of all events and the interest of the
readers of the newspaper in them, though the latter point is
overemphasized on most newspapers.   These matters all
enter in when an editor is considering the balance to be
given to the.day's news, how much space is to be devoted
to certain stories, whether certain other stories shall be
cut down or left out altogether.

However objective a man (or woman) may strive to be,
he is likely to be misled at a critical moment by his own
philosophy of life or his own private interests unless he is
guided by some definite standard.   Consequently, in order
to insure fairness in handling and balancing the news, some
newspapers have—and probably all should have—specific
rules as to what sort of news must be printed.   In a large
city all cases filed in a court of a certain rank must, according to such rules, be dealt with in the news columns.   The
smaller the city, the lower the jurisdiction of the court
whose proceedings must be chronicled.   In the small town,
however, there is a strong tendency for the editor to suppress unpleasant news altogether, on the specious ground
that publication will do harm to the individual involved or
more often to the individual's family, but in reality, as was
pointed out in a previous chapter,[1] because the editor is
afraid.

The rationalization offered in this attitude is well answered by William Allen White in discussing a specific
case, that of the drunkard: "The man who fills up with
whiskey and goes about making a fool of himself, becomes
a public nuisance.   If permitted to continue it, he becomes
a public charge.   The public has an interest in him.   Publicity is one of the things that keeps him straight.   His

[1] See p. 92.

first offense is ignored in *The Gazette,* but his second offense is recorded when he is arrested, and no matter how high or low he is, his name goes in. We have printed this warning to drinkers time and again; so when they come around asking us to think of their wives and children, or their sick mothers or poor old fathers, we always tell them to remember that they had fair warning, and if their fathers and mothers and wives and children are nothing to them before taking, they are nothing to us after taking." [1]

A frequent argument in favor of suppression of the news of crime or vice in a small town is that its publication destroys the reputation of the town outside, and, furthermore, stirs up ill feeling in the town itself. The same argument would, if carried to a logical conclusion, prevent a clergyman from preaching against evil and even a court from punishing it. It is based, consciously or unconsciously, on the doctrine that whatever is concealed can do no harm. It is, moreover, the argument regularly advanced by the friends and supporters of professional gamblers, thugs, and other criminals in endeavoring to prevent a city from being cleaned up. Newspapers which adopt this reasoning are merely playing into the hands of criminal and degenerate elements of the public.

As Mr. White points out, news of crime or misdemeanor is a public matter and publicity is a deterrent to evil-doing. Furthermore, particularly in the small town, publicity affords a measure of protection to the evil-doer himself against exaggeration of the evil that he has committed. If the facts are left unpublished, town gossip will exaggerate them out of all proportion to their actual state. The publication of the exact facts enables the public to obtain a correct understanding and to draw fair conclusions from it.

[1] Quoted by J. S. Myers in *The Journalistic Code of Ethics,* p. 30.

In certain small towns and even in large cities, news is sometimes suppressed because of the prominence of the persons involved. In the cities, however, newspaper competition has largely eliminated this condition and most metropolitan dailies will publish the news of a minor offense of which a prominent person is accused, while omitting reference to the same offense if committed by an obscure individual. The reason is that the doings of persons of prominence are held to be of public interest and in some degree of public importance. While this point of view is open to question, there is some argument to justify it. Any prominence which a person has attained, he has attained through society. Recognition obtained by wealth, by family position, or by ability, is obtained from society and by reason of living in a state of society. Society may be said to possess a greater interest in the individual whom it has thus recognized than in the person who has achieved no prominence.

Many newspapers have rules providing for the omission of certain matters of news. These may be divided into two classes: (1) Matters which are suppressed out of consideration for the individual concerned; and (2) matters suppressed for the general interests of society.

Under the first head come offenses of women and children. Many papers have a rule against publishing the proceedings of juvenile courts with the name of the individuals involved, unless the proceedings involve a sentence to a reform school or some other place of correction. Justification for this is given by a statute in many states, such statutes making the juvenile court a partly judicial tribunal, while in part the juvenile court stands *in loco parentis* to the child, giving advice and counsel and even administering corporal punishment. For this reason, the hearings of juvenile courts are often made private by statute, the reason for public court trials, the preservation of the integrity and reputation of the judiciary, being not here involved. Where no sentence is imposed, it is obviously better for the child and in no way harmful to society that his playmates should not have the opportunity to ridicule him or to make a hero of him. Childhood is essentially sensitive, and to it the wages of sin may not properly be publicity.

Cases involving women involve a somewhat similar point of view. While clear-thinking people recognize that it ought not to be so, the fact remains that in our present civilization a woman finds it difficult to regain a reputation lost through lack of chastity. Even where no want of chastity on the part of the woman herself is involved, she is often affected by being involuntarily involved in some unfortunate situation, as in the case of the girl referred to in Masters's *Spoon River Anthology*.[1] For this reason hearings in the so-called morals courts of cities are not infrequently private. Practically all newspapers enjoin greater care in dealing with the reputation of women, and many of them have a specific rule that the names of women shall not be mentioned in cases involving apparent want of chastity unless the woman is a prostitute or the case presents other aspects of importance. In respect to all other crimes and offenses, women stand on the same plane as men so far as publication of news in the average paper is concerned. Possibly the average reporter exercises a little more care—in some cases his paper instructs him to do so—in dealing with news about women. This, of course, is an unjustifiable position, for he should exercise the maximum of care in dealing with news about all persons.

In the other class of details commonly omitted are in-

[1] See poem, *Nellie Clark*.

cluded such matters as the names of poisons used in committing suicide, the specific methods employed by burglars in executing their crimes, and the salacious details of abnormal crimes. The reason for the suppression of these facts is simply that they are likely to be suggestive to the psychopathic or the criminal. It has been found that the publication of stories of the use of a certain poison for committing suicide is followed by a large number of suicides in the same manner. The evidence as to criminal acts is less definite.

That not all newspapers suppress details of this sort is evident. For instance, a metropolitan daily purported to tell how a young burglar had bungled in committing his first job and how he might have avoided capture.[1] Presumably in this case the young reporter was merely anxious to air his supposititious knowledge of the tactics of burglars or to be amusing and the item slipped past the copy desk unchanged.

Certain newspapers lay great stress on language as an ethical matter. The writer knows of one newspaper which flagrantly colors its news, in some cases completely misrepresenting the facts, but which makes a great point of barring from its columns all profanity, even such words as "damn." Many newspapers, in an effort to appear moral, use words which the middle class assumes represent better ethical standards. For example, a woman is always said to "disrobe," never "undress," although the latter word is both colloquially and in literature practically universal. Such practices simply represent a confusion of morality and convention.

About the foregoing matters definite rules can be laid down. So far as real progress is concerned, they are

---

[1] See story, *Tried to Rob Uncle's Home, The Kansas City Star,* February 25, 1920.

relatively unimportant. They are the more trivial matters of news.

In the larger matters of news no set rules can be laid down. As matter falls into more definite classes and is more efficiently recorded, the problem of suppression will grow less. A sound ethical rule that the newspaper can follow at present with reference to suppressing matter is never to suppress any matter because of its connection with a private interest, because of its unpleasantness to the editor, because of doubt as to whether the public should have the information, or for any other reason than a conviction that it is of less importance than other news available. In the balancing of the news is a great test of the journalist's objectivity of vision. It is here in particular that the journalist who is full of opinion instead of fact will unconsciously betray his public. Against this no one can guard him carefully, for there is no one but is prone to lapses from objectivity.

Additional Readings

Bennett, *What the Public Wants.*

Symposium: Giving the Public What it Wants, in Thorpe's *The Coming Newspaperman,* pp. 223–247.

William Rockhill Nelson: The Story of a Man, a Newspaper, and a City, pp. 115–133.

Lippmann, *Public Opinion,* pp. 338–357.

Scott-James, *The Influence of the Press,* pp. 157–174.

VII

The Principle of Objectivity Applied: Sensationalism

Sensationalism in the press, particularly the daily press, presents as acute practical problems to the editor as does any phase of giving due proportion to the news. Sensationalism is in part a phase of proportion in the news, for if it does nothing else, it emphasizes certain news facts to the exclusion or the minimizing of others. Again, the problems of sensationalism involve the business interests of the newspaper even more directly than does any problem of news suppression, for the readers of not a few newspapers, trained to care for sensational journalism, have little taste for anything better. There also is involved in sensationalism the ethical question as to the desirability of "playing up" criminal, vicious, or sordid sides of life.

Certain common factors of sensationalism are simple matters. The manufacture of news, misrepresentation, coloring, are to be condemned outright. They are as reprehensible when used for sensational purposes, merely to titillate the nerves of readers, as when used for the definite purpose of conveying false information about important affairs. There is no ethical difference between lying about a divorce case in order to arouse the sensational interest of readers and lying about a strike in order to protect private interests. Direct misrepresentation for the purpose of being sensational is not so common as it once was, but it is still too common.

The war with Spain in 1898 was to a considerable extent attributable to the efforts of sensational newspapers. Their desire for war was apparently based neither on a conviction that the United States had a righteous cause nor on a desire to increase the profits or prestige of America. Their desire seemed to be mainly to write good stories, which a war would enable them to do. In July, 1919, according to the Chicago Commission on Race Relations, *The Herald-Examiner* published a story about several thousand men breaking into the Eighth Regiment armory to seize guns and ammunition, with police action and casualties. The Commission states that there were no weapons in the armory, that it was not broken into, though some windows were broken, and that there was no such clash with the police.[1] Other Chicago papers were criticized by the Commission for sensational and inflammatory reports of the rioting that occurred in the summer of 1919 between negroes and whites.[2] While the difficulty of obtaining accurate news at the time is recognized, the increased responsibility of the press in periods of popular hysteria is stressed.

Not infrequently misrepresentation is the fault of reporters who, in the absence of instructions from their paper or even counter to such instructions, write sensational stories in the hope, often justified, that it will enhance their value to the paper. Such reporters have no sense of honor, and their superiors too often excuse themselves by laying the whole blame upon the reporter while accepting the reporter's story.

The invasion of privacy for sensational reasons is another practice which cannot be condoned. It is necessary,

[1] *The Negro in Chicago,* p. 29.
[2] *Idem.,* pp. 25–33.

of course, to consider carefully what proper privacy is. The young reporter is often too willing to refrain from writing justifiable news because he is persuaded by some person of prominence that it is none of the paper's business. Matters which are of importance to the public welfare are the public's business and the reporter has a right to obtain them in any honorable way he can. He is under no obligation to wait until some interested person has used these facts for his private gain and has then determined to release them officially to the press. Indeed, he is under obligation not to wait until that time, provided he can get the facts in an honorable manner with a certainty that they are facts. Most of the facts which are of concern to the public, persons directly concerned with them are unwilling to reveal or are willing to reveal only equivocally or inadequately. No one objects to the revelation of such facts except those who desire to conceal from the public those facts to which it is entitled.

The invasion of privacy to which objection is justifiably made by all right-thinking persons is that which drags into the limelight of publicity persons, particularly women, who are indirectly connected with news of sensational interest. For example, a young woman of doubtful reputation is murdered. The authorities announce that they plan to question a wealthy and prominent married man who was intimately acquainted with her. Under pressure from the press the authorities reveal the name of this man. So far the press has performed a service. The public is entitled to know who this man is and the authorities are properly compelled to act as representatives of the people and not as private inquisitors seeking to protect individuals because of their wealth and position. Following this, however, newspapers seek out the wife of this man, attempt to subject her to questioning which can have no possible concern to the public, even spy upon her home to such an extent that it is necessary for her to post guards to obtain ordinary privacy. The papers publish what they can obtain about her, including her photograph. The purpose of this is purely to appeal to the morbid and sentimental curiosity of a certain group of readers. In doing this the newspaper has deserted its function as a purveyor of accurate news and has become a cheap society gossip. It is a happy augury that an incident of precisely this character was vigorously condemned recently by the *Editor and Publisher,* which represents the best newspaper standards of the country.[1]

The practice complained of, however, is common even among newspapers which are not ultra-sensational. The publication of photographs of relatives of criminals, the use of interviews with persons whose only connection with news is through some other individual, and many similar practices may be observed in the press every day.

So much for such factors in sensationalism as are not justified from any point of view. Nobody justifies them, not even those who perpetrate them.

Eliminating misrepresentation of all kinds and invasion of privacy, the problem of sensationalism resolves itself largely into a question of balance. As has been pointed out before, it is utterly unjustifiable to carry out the process of news selection either in the paper as a whole or in individual stories in such a way as to conceal from the people facts of importance to their welfare. Even without any intention of concealment, however, a newspaper may adopt widely varying policies with reference to selecting news. The newspaper which appeals to intellectual people makes

[1] *And They Called It Journalism, Editor and Publisher.* March 31, 1923, p. 34.

its selection primarily on the basis of importance. At the opposite pole are the ultra-sensational newspapers which make their selection on the basis purely of interest—what is popularly termed "human interest," the same interest that causes people to turn to popular novels and to see melodrama on the stage. The development of the theory of "human interest" as a criterion in news selection came chiefly with the building of large circulations by sensational newspapers, particularly the earlier Hearst papers, in the great cities. These papers built their initial circulations among groups of the population which previously had not read any newspaper. These people belonged to the working class and were not more than a generation or two removed from Europe. They had little knowledge of political, economic, or social problems in the United States. Their interests were narrowed to their homes, their shops, and a few familiar haunts. A sensational criminal trial aroused their attention much more than a war between Japan and Russia or a steel strike in Pennsylvania. Give them what they want, the newspaper publishers decreed, and thus the "human interest" newspaper developed.

While it may be said in behalf of the sensational newspapers that they educated a relatively ignorant group of the population in the practice of newspaper reading, it is also true that the sensational press has influenced every section of American journalism. W. R. Nelson, the veteran publisher of *The Kansas City Star*, used to assert that the trouble with most editors is that they allow Mr. Hearst to run their papers.

The influence of the sensational journals on other sections of the press has been most marked in two respects. One of these has been overemphasized by critics to an extreme extent. That is the development of the large headline. This does not necessarily have any ethical import whatsoever, and care must always be taken to distinguish between ethics and taste. The only possible harm that the large headline may intrinsically do, from an ethical standpoint, is to crowd out news that otherwise would be printed. The large headline was devised by sensational newspapers to attract readers. It is used today for the same purpose by all newspapers that use it at all. It possesses particular commercial value for street and newsstand sales. It is not necessarily a mark of sensationalism. Some newspapers that are very conservative in their investigating and writing of news use large headlines. Some other newspapers that treat stories in a highly sensational manner put small headlines over them—in some instances for the probable purpose of impressing the conservative-minded but ignorant reader, who because of the early use of scare-heads by "yellow" journals draws conclusions as to the accuracy of the story in inverse proportion to the size of the head. So far as indicating the relative importance of news stories is concerned, this can be accomplished by the relative size of the heads, irrespective of the actual type sizes employed. It may be questioned, moreover, whether indication of the relative importance of news stories is really desirable, since it constitutes essentially an interpretation on the part of the editor and removes the reader one step further from strict objective facts. Contemporary readers, accustomed to spending but a small amount of time on their newspaper,[1] would doubtless be unready, however, for this practice to be changed.

The other form of influence of sensational journalism on

[1] An investigation conducted by Walter Dill Scott indicated that the typical Chicago business or professional man spent fifteen minutes a day reading local newspapers. See Scott, *The Psychology of Advertising*, pp. 375–394.

the American press in general is much more significant, although less attention has been paid to it by critics. That
influence is in the direction of emphasizing interest rather
than importance as a test of news. In doing this, the sensational newspapers simply appeal to an ancient and powerful
instinct. As John Macy says, "Everybody likes a story,
and there are only a few souls in the world who yearn at
breakfast for information." [1] The sinister side of the situation is found in the fact that sensational newspapers and
the other journals that followed their example merely took,
for the most part, the stories that lay ready to their hands,
which meant the trivial, the purely entertaining, the ephemeral. The effect of this practice is seen in the manner in
which the Dempsey-Gibbons fight and the convention of
the National Education Association were covered by the
press of the United States in the summer of 1923. The
newspapers of representative American cities on July 5 devoted the following number of column inches to the two
events respectively: [2]

	Fight	Convention
New York	1,425¾	93½
Chicago	1,353½	1¾
Washington	405	8

What American newspapers might have done in the past,
and what they may still do, is to make the really important
so thoroughly intelligible that it cannot fail to be of interest.
That this can be done is shown by the experience of

[1] *Civilization in the United States*, p. 45.
[2] Figures from *The Christian Science Monitor*, July 6, 1923. In Boston
The Monitor and *The Transcript* devoted respectively 0 and 25½ inches to
the fight, 227 and 40 inches to the convention. *The Post, The Globe,* and
The Herald ignored the convention but gave a total of 942½ inches to the
fight.

Science Service in making scientific material, usually considered the height of dullness, interesting to the average reader. It is not easy to make the important intelligible, and perhaps the chief harm that has been done by sensationalism consists in its regularly having taken the easiest way to the interests of readers. If the practice grows of making the important interesting, the ultimate influence of sensational journalism will prove a happy one, in that it will be found to have been the indirect cause of creating an interest in the important in the large body of persons who read only for interest and entertainment.

In justice to the sensational press, one should recognize the fact that it has done some good in stimulating reporting. It has made investigation by reporters a part of the day's work. While the investigations undertaken by sensational newspapers have not always been of the right character, they have shown the opportunity and duty of the press as an investigating force. On no paper of consequence is the reporter any longer merely a listener.

There is further to be considered the fact of sensationalism in its influence upon the ethical standards and practices of newspaper readers. The treatment of the news of crime and vice affords a fair opportunity to examine different standards of policy and practice on the part of the press as respects sensationalism. At one extreme stand those who would exclude all, or practically all, news of crime and vice on the ground that it can do no possible good to the readers to have these things brought to their attention. This view finds few supporters among members of the profession of journalism. Its only newspaper representative in this country is *The Christian Science Monitor*, which, moreover, does not absolutely exclude all news of crime. Furthermore, this paper differs from other newspapers in being not primarily a local but an international paper. *The Christian Science Monitor,* the bulk of whose circulation is outside the vicinity of Boston, where it is published, stands in a relation wholly different from the ordinary newspaper whose circulation, even in the case of the most conspicuous American papers, is confined largely to the trading area of its city.

Next there is a group of newspapers, small in number, represented by such a paper as *The Boston Evening Transcript,* which deal very briefly with news of crime. A sensational murder in Boston received in *The Transcript* two inches of type under a two-deck head, as against more than three columns, under a streamer head and illustrated by two photographs, in a sensational Boston newspaper. It is argued in behalf of *The Transcript's* way of handling news of crime that the public is entitled to the news and that it is a safeguard to the ethical welfare of the community and the administration of justice that publicity be given to crime, but that extensive details of crime are demoralizing and debasing.

The bulk of the larger newspapers of the country belong to two other groups, one of them giving news of crime in detail but balancing it with other news to varying extent, the other "playing up" the news of crime with sensational and often suggestive details. In behalf of both of these practices and more particularly the latter, the argument is advanced that while the prevention and punishment of crime are the responsibility of the public the public must be startled into attention to crime. It is to be feared that in most instances this argument is a rationalization invented to account for playing up crime in order to appeal to the morbid sensibilities of the reader, of the writer, or of both.

In cases where the newspaper might perform a service

by publishing detailed news of crime, it commonly destroys its effectiveness by adopting the psychology and clamor of the mob. For example, when sex crimes occur, the average newspaper and the average reader shout such terms as "fiend" and "degeneracy." They feel the common repugnance to the unnatural or the abnormal, and see in persons guilty of sex crimes a wilful moral guilt. As a matter of fact, sex crimes are almost invariably the result of definitely recognized psychopathies.

It is an astounding fact that in the various trials in which Harry K. Thaw was involved and concerning which certain newspapers published such revolting details that they were threatened with criminal prosecution, no newspaper or magazine, to the writer's knowledge, published a sound, understandable explanation of the sexual psychopathy with which Thaw was and is afflicted, or discussed the means of guarding against the menace of this condition in human life.

Again, in all the stories that appeared in Kansas City papers in 1921 concerning a "vice ring" in that city, there was line after line of suggestive material that might easily cause a boy or girl to wish to delve further into the type of vice represented, but there was not a line in any newspaper in that city that gave a rational explanation of the sexual inversion with which the leaders of this ring were afflicted, or the proper psychiatric method of handling such cases. Without such explanation, the news was really incomplete.

Whether sensational news in general is to any considerable extent promotive of crime or vice is a debatable question, with the direct evidence largely negative. On the other hand, it is often argued by moralists that sensational news produces a general weakening of the moral fiber and a general lowering of ethical standards. In opposition to this point of view, it is pointed out that such weakening and lowering, if they exist, are as probably the causes as the results of sensationalism. Again, it must be borne in mind that much of the objection to sensationalism is esthetic rather than ethical, even though considered by the objectors to be the latter.

It is evident that sensational news crowds out other news, often of much greater importance. Not only the emphasis on crime and vice, but the attention to trivialities, characteristic of sensational journalism, means less space for significant news. If a paper devotes a column to describing the contents of forty-seven trunks of clothing owned by a musical comedy star or to telling how firemen spent half an hour rescuing a cat marooned on a telephone pole, international and national news is bound to suffer.

The newspaper, of course, must be interesting if it is to attract readers, and unless it attracts readers it serves no social purpose. On the other hand, it must convey facts of importance if it is to be of public value. How far the public is naturally devoted to the trivial and sensational, and to what extent it has been turned in these directions by newspaper efforts, is an open question, as is also the problem of how far any given newspaper can go in eliminating the trivial and continue to please the general reader, to whom the average newspaper must make its appeal. There is an occasional city in which there is a sufficient clientele of well-educated, cultured readers to support an almost purely informative newspaper. This is not true of the average American city or town. There are few places in which a paper like *The Boston Evening Transcript*, with no sensational news, with a circulation slightly in excess of 30,000, and with an advertising rate of 20 cents per agate line, could be successfully run.

On the other hand, it is not necessary to maintain a

sensational newspaper in order to compete successfully with the sensational press. This is merely the easiest thing to do. The public prefers the material with which the sensational press deals because it is easy to understand and because it furnishes an emotional outlet, through its human interest. Human interest and emotional quality can, however, be put into news of importance. The relation of the important to everyday life can be made clear. The reason why this is not generally done is that most authorities on subjects of importance are dull speakers and writers, while few newspapers have reporters or editors who can so translate this material as to make an intellectual and emotional appeal to the general public. The growth of *The Kansas City Star*, one of the most striking in American journalism, was due largely to its owner's policy of selecting from other publications matters of importance and at the same time of public interest. Under this policy the paper, largely devoid of sensationalism, competed successfully with highly sensational publications and maintained a larger subscription list and a heavier run of advertising.

In the small town the problem of sensationalism does not enter to any considerable extent. The small town newspaper is tending to become more and more a local publication. Its telegraph service, if any, is meager. Readers who desire the sensational obtain it in metropolitan dailies published in a city nearby. Little that is of itself sensational occurs in the average small town. When it does happen, it is not likely to be sensationally treated. This is due partly to lack of training in sensational writing on the part of local newspapermen. It is in part due to lack of public demand for the sensational. Moreover, the individual in the small town is likely to see the importance to himself of matters of public interest in the community.

Public attention, so far as the newspapers are concerned, is therefore centered in matters of some significance. Furthermore, the backyard gossip, which occupies a considerable place in sensational dailies in metropolitan centers, is retailed in the small town by word of mouth—which of course is no improvement over its publication by a newspaper except that the latter practice gives it a seemingly more vital relation to the social structure.

Unquestionably, the tide of sensationalism has begun to recede. The demand for a saner ideal for the press is manifest among both newspapermen and readers. For example, the women of Los Angeles started early in 1923 a movement for less emphasis on crime and scandal in the newspapers of southern California.[1] As an instance of the attitude of editors and publishers may be cited the resolution adopted by the Oregon Editorial Association in 1922:

"Whereas, We believe that the newspaper profession is one of the most honorable, the most influential, and most important of the professions and should therefore be the most careful of all of them in maintaining high ideals of service, promoting a high consideration for public and private morals; and

"Whereas, We are convinced that too much stress laid upon scandals, crimes, and stories of immorality has a bad influence upon the public mind, especially upon those minds that are young and impressionable; therefore, be it

"Resolved, That while we recognize the duty devolving upon a newspaper to publish the news, in reference to these matters, yet we urge that salacious details be not overemphasized and we especially urge the various press associations to refrain from unduly emphasizing this class of news in their dispatches."

[1] See news story, *300,000 California Citizens Demand Cleaner Newspapers*, and editorial, *The Call for Clean Journalism, The Christian Science Monitor*, January 6, 1923.

Additional Readings

Chicago Commission on Race Relations, *The Negro in Chicago,* pp. 436–594.

Street, *The Truth About the Newspaper. Chicago Tribune,* July 25, 1909.

Fenton, *The Influence of Newspaper Presentation upon the Growth of Crime and Other Anti-Social Activity. American Journal of Sociology* 16:342–371, 538–564.

Alger, *Sensational Journalism and the Law,* in Bleyer's *The Profession of Journalism,* pp. 167–180.

Lloyd, *Newspaper Conscience—A Study in Half-Truths. American Journal of Sociology* 27: 197–210.

Gladden, *Tainted Journalism: Good and Bad,* in Thorpe's *The Coming Newspaper,* pp. 27–50.

And They Called It Journalism. Editor and Publisher, March 31, 1923, p. 34.

Scott, *The Psychology of Advertising,* pp. 375–394.

The Call for Clean Journalism and *300,000 California Citizens Demand Cleaner Newspapers. The Christian Science Monitor,* January 6, 1923.

Williams, *Presidential Address,* in *The Press Congress of the World in Hawaii,* pp. 70–77.

VIII

THE PRINCIPLE OF OBJECTIVITY APPLIED: EDITORIAL LEADERSHIP

With the emphasis that has been laid on objectivity as the primary ideal of the newspaper, the question naturally arises: Is there no place in modern journalism for editorial leadership?

Few journalists or students of public opinion would now maintain that a newspaper is under any obligation to furnish editorial guidance of any sort to its readers.   They hold that the ideal of molding public opinion has been largely supplanted by the ideal of disseminating objective facts.   Some, perhaps, chiefly among the older men, look back with regret to the old days.   Others, holding very modern, realistic views, question whether any molding of public opinion is desirable in a country maintaining a popular government.

The majority, while not regarding editorial guidance as by any means the most significant function of the press, maintain that it still occupies a place among the proper functions of journalism.   Few papers are ready to abandon it.   There are, however, a number of country weeklies without editorial pages, and there is occasionally a country weekly with an editor of sufficient courage to publish an editorial only when he feels he has something definitely worth saying to his community.   Practically no newspapers of metropolitan dimensions are without editorial pages.

The influence exerted by the press through editorial comment appears to be diminishing. Observers point to elections in New York City in which candidates were elected against the opposition of all the newspapers or against the opposition of all but two or three. They point to similar conditions in Kansas City. They note that the two most recently elected governors of Oklahoma and Kansas were chosen against the advice of an overwhelming majority of the newspapers. No one who has taken account of conditions like these can believe that the editorial influence of the press is as potent as its wide distribution might make plausible.

One reason for the waning editorial influence of the press is the fact that the public has become convinced that in controversial matters, especially partisan politics, the news furnished by the press is not dependable. The public reasons that if the press will lie in its news columns the reasoning in the editorial columns cannot be depended upon. It is true that considerations of this sort do not affect the great body of partisan voters, who cling to their own party with an inertia which nothing can overcome. It does, however, influence the independent voters, who are almost always a minority but who are in sufficient numbers in most places to hold the balance of power in elections.

A further reason for the defeat of the press in elections and the waning public confidence which this indicates, is the fact that the press is disposed to critical comment chiefly at election times. This convinces the public that the press is interested in winning elections rather than in advocating policies of public benefit. A newspaper which steadily, in season and out of season, advocates the policies in which it believes and calls attention to acts of public officials for and against these policies, has a much better chance of being influential with American voters.

It is often asserted that the editorial page of a newspaper is less read than was formerly the case. If one considers the proportion of readers who consult the editorial page, the statement is true; if one considers the actual number, it is untrue. Early newspapers were taken by a small minority of the public. At the close of the War of 1812 no New York newspaper had a circulation of more than 2,000.[1] In those days practically all the subscribers read everything in the paper. The paper was small enough and subscribers had leisure enough to permit of this. The newspaper readers of that day, however, represented an extremely small minority of the voting public, although probably they had greater influence than a similar group would have today.

Today practically every literate citizen living where a daily paper is readily available, reads one. The majority give little or no attention to the editorial page. The common estimate is that twenty per cent of the readers of a metropolitan daily read the editorials, while a somewhat larger proportion take some interest in the editorial page as a whole. They may care for the humorous column, for the correspondence department, or for some other editorial page feature. It still remains true that the more intellectual and influential persons read the editorials, although they are tending to accept the guidance of the weekly journals of opinion rather than that of the newspapers. The number of these readers in proportion to the population is much greater than it was one hundred or even fifty years ago. The editorial department of the paper is getting as wide a hearing as ever and, for the most part, among pre-

[1] Lee, *History of American Journalism*, p. 142.

cisely those persons who are independent in their voting and their views.

In an effort still further to enlarge the circulation of readers of editorial matter, a number of newspapers have adopted the policy of publishing editorials on the front page, either regularly, as with the columns contributed by Arthur Brisbane to the Hearst newspapers, or occasionally, as with the editorial published on the front page in *The Kansas City Star* at times when the staff of the paper feels that there is an issue which deserves this position.

A number of papers are publishing signed columns expressing personal editorial convictions. It is somewhat questionable whether the signed editorial exerts any more influence than the unsigned one. Precisely those papers which use signed editorials are well known to the public to represent specific private ownership. Everyone who would be influenced by the signature at the bottom of an editorial knows that the Hearst newspapers represent the personality and views of Mr. Hearst, even though they may be technically owned by a corporation. Even if they did not know this fact, the probability is that the public would not be any more influenced by the signature of a writer, unless he were nationally known, than by an expression of opinion on the part of the paper. It is true that newspaper editors, if they signed their editorials, would become better known among the reading public and this would probably be advantageous for newspapers. Certainly it would be desirable, from the reader's point of view and probably the newspaper's also, to print the names of the editorial council at the masthead of the paper. The journals of opinion now do this, with much enhancement of prestige thereby.

There are certain advantages, however, in a newspaper's speaking as an institution. The larger metropolitan dailies all have editorial councils which meet daily. At these meetings all possible subjects for editorials are discussed, and it is decided what editorials shall be written. Except on the most highly technical matters the general position to be taken is also determined, after considerable discussion. The decision may be made by vote or, more commonly, by the official head of the paper. Assignments of editorials to be written are then made to the various editorial writers. No writer is ever asked to write an editorial which does violence to his own convictions. If the writer to whom a particular editorial would normally be assigned feels that he cannot conscientiously write it in accordance with the decision of the editorial council, it is assigned to some one else. Such a situation, of course, rarely arises, because the members of the editorial council of a newspaper are likely to have similar views; the newspaper employs men who are in general accord with its policy. A conservative newspaper has an editorial council made up of conservatives; and in like manner, the editorial council of a liberal journal is regularly made up of liberals. The editorials resulting from an editorial council, while they are written by individuals, do not represent merely individual views, but these views modified and added to by the convictions of other members of the council.

On the smaller papers, where all the editorial writing is done by one person, that person may come into conflict often enough with the publisher of the paper unless, as rarely happens, he and the publisher have precisely the same notions of public policies. On a British newspaper the editor would be supreme.[1] On an American newspaper, unfortunately, this is not the case. But any editorial

[1] This is the time-honored practice. But, in contrast, see Belloc's *The Free Press.*

writer had better resign than write what he considers to be false. By writing editorials in which he does not believe, he betrays his employer by turning out copy that does not have the ring of conviction, and the public by misrepresenting what he conceives to be the actual situation.

On the still smaller papers, where the publisher writes his own editorials, he is responsible only to his own conscience as a public servant. In most cases he is insufficiently qualified to discuss national or international issues intelligently, but he may effectively lead his community in community affairs. In contrast to metropolitan dailies, a small-town daily or weekly is often the greatest single influence in the community. Here are both responsibility and privilege.

The editorial writer, on whatever paper, should have as his primary function clarifying facts and helping readers to draw dependable conclusions from the facts. More and more is it being recognized that the editorial is an interpreter more than an advocate. It combines in one the parts of public prosecutor, public defender, and judge What a responsibility rests upon it, therefore, not to misrepresent in the slightest degree any fact which it may have obtained from the news or elsewhere and to make use of no specious arguments in drawing its conclusions. That such arguments are used by editors, there is no doubt. On the other hand, in many cases they are employed unconsciously. The writer is misled by his prejudices, his fears, and his hopes, or perhaps he is incapable, as many reasonably competent writers are, of sound, logical reasoning.

In many instances an integral part of the newspaper's editorial influence is found in so-called "editorial campaigns." These, because of the iteration that they involve, produce more apparent results, at least for the time being,

than do editorial efforts in general. Examples are the crusade of *The Chicago Tribune* for a sane Fourth of July,
begun by James Keeley in 1899 and brought to fruition in
recent years in the all-but-universal ban on private use of
fireworks [1] ; and the campaign of *The New York Tribune*
to stamp out fraudulent advertising, which was not carried
on vigorously for a sufficient time to bring as notable results.[2] Like other editorial leadership, such campaigns in
general do not constitute an ethical obligation of the press;
a newspaper is free to be a "crusading newspaper" or not,
as it chooses.

It is not true, however, that there are no circumstances
under which the fundamentals of a campaign are strictly
matters of news and consequently facts which a newspaper
is ethically bound to present to its readers. This was the
situation when *The New York Times,* not normally a "crusading newspaper," exposed the Tweed Ring in 1870–71.
Less obviously a matter of news, though still very close to
it, was the exposé by *The Detroit News* of fake race track
gambling in 1922. It must be apparent here that the
writer holds a somewhat broader view of news than is held
by some critics, notably Mr. Walter Lippmann, who maintains that "the function of news is [exclusively] to signalize
an event." [3] While there is much justice in his contention
that news is too often regarded merely as another word for
truth and consequently impossible demands are made of the
press, hardly any journalist of adequate experience in dealing with news would be willing to restrict the term as Mr.
Lippmann does. The practiced journalist realizes that at

[1] See *The W. G. N.*, p. 60, for details.
[2] The methods of the campaign are discussed in the *Tribune* pamphlet,
How It Works, and examples may be found by consulting the files of
The Ad-Visor column in *The Tribune* in 1914–1916.
[3] *Public Opinion,* p. 358.

times the absence of an event is as important news as an event itself. In the case of the Tweed Ring, the campaign of *The New York Times* really began with publication of the fact that the financial accounts of the city were being concealed in spite of the law making them public property. The failure of the municipal officials to publish any financial statement was, in the opinion of the writer, news. A critic with Mr. Lippmann's point of view would doubtless maintain that no news existed until some citizen should, for instance, bring mandamus proceedings to compel the opening of the books to the public. With the multiplicity of efforts made to conceal from the press what is obviously news, it seems hardly practicable for the reporter to desert the investigative function. If he does desert it, the published news will become more and more inconsequential.

In the fact that matters commonly assigned to the province of the "crusade" are often closely associated with news, there is an element of danger to sound ethical practice. Whenever an institution, such as the press, or, for that matter, an individual, embarks on a campaign for what is conceived to be for human betterment, there appears the tendency to emphasize facts that support the desired end, to minimize facts that seem to oppose it, and even to falsify the actual situation altogether. At present these practices are evident in newspapers which are campaigning for the abandonment or reduction of prohibition and likewise in journals which are advocating "bone-dry" measures. In any campaign in which it is interested, and particularly in any which it has itself inaugurated, a newspaper must walk delicately and circumspectly if it is not to be condemned as a follower of the doctrine that the end justifies the means.

Apart from news matters, the ethical position which one will take on campaigns by a newspaper will depend largely on his views on social institutions generally. The journalist is likely to see in such service a certain danger to the supremacy of news in the function of the press. He has observed that papers which devote great attention to crusades commonly devote correspondingly less space and attention to news. Even if campaigns did not interfere with news in this respect, they would nevertheless tend, he feels, to distract the citizen's attention from so digesting objective facts as to be able to accomplish for himself, by ballot and other legitimate means, what the newspaper attempts to do for him.

Loose, sentimental idealism, both within and without the newspaper office, is inclined naturally toward a vast number of campaigns and a vast amount of special service of all sorts. "Anything that is for the public good should be done by the press," represents fairly this undiscriminating attitude. The sensational press has emphasized campaigns and other special service to readers, partly, no doubt, for commercial reasons, partly because of a desire to put "human interest" into the newspaper, to make it, in the words of a prominent exemplar of this type of journalism, "a paper with a heart and a soul." It cannot be denied that special service does put readers into human touch with the newspaper. The same is true of any conspicuous editorial leadership. The development of such a situation is useful to the publication both in giving weight to its editorial utterances and in establishing credence for its news. The average person takes his views, and even his "facts," from those whom he admires. As Dr. Sigmund Freud says:

"Faith repeats the history of its own origin; it is a derivative of love and at first requires no arguments. When they are offered by a beloved person, arguments may later be admitted and subjected to critical reflection. Arguments without such support avail nothing, and never mean anything in life to most persons. Man's intellect is accessible only so far as he is capable of libidinous occupation with an object." [1]

The fact here brought out should make the newspaper which has attained public confidence and affection by special service or any other means, doubly careful not to violate that confidence by misrepresentation of news or specious editorial argument.

Closely allied to editorial leadership on the part of a newspaper, one is likely to find the expression—as distinguished from the molding—of public opinion. The correspondence column, by whatever name called, offers this opportunity. It serves a less important function than many suppose, for contributions come to it from an extremely small minority of the public, not infrequently those whose opinions are highly colored by the fact that their personal interests are involved in the points at issue.

In the handling of letters submitted for publication the honest editor is scrupulously careful. He is under no obligation to print a letter because some reader writes it. He has the right to use his own judgment. He is under obligation, however, to correct any error which he has made and which has been brought by a reader to his attention. He is unfair to his readers if, in publishing letters in his correspondence department, he does not give fair balance to the various sides represented. It is wholly unethical for him to publish numerous letters which commend his own point of view and to omit those letters which differ from that point of view.

[1] *A General Introduction to Psychoanalysis*, p. 385.

Still more unethical is it for an editor so to edit or head a letter that it will convey an impression opposite to or even different from that which the writer intended. It is frequently complained that editors do this. For example, Professor Alfred H. Lloyd calls attention to an incident in which he himself figured:

"Not long ago I sent a communication to a paper of different political views from my own. The letter was an experiment. It called attention to a certain public man's opportunism and inconsistencies, quoting his speeches at different times. I wondered if the paper would publish the letter and face the exposure. It did publish the letter, but with saving headlines, and I have to add, with editorial omissions of essential sentences, so that a shifting and truth-careless politician was made to seem a patriot! I was, of course, helpless. The paper had a right, at least a legal right, so long as newspapers are not common carriers or public servants, not to publish at all, but it had no right either to its headlines or to the editorial changes." [1]

Not infrequently, of course, a letter containing material that a newspaper would like to publish is too long. Condensation is always dangerous. Elisions are less dangerous if made with care and honesty. No newspaper may justifiably cut a letter without indicating the places at which it made elisions. The danger in honest elision is that unconsciously the editor may omit significant material and thus commit an unethical act, or may omit passages which are not really significant but which the writer of the letter thinks are, and may thus gain with that writer and among his friends a reputation for unethical conduct, which is just as detrimental to the standing of a newspaper as unethical

[1] *The American Journal of Sociology*, vol. 27, p. 203.

conduct itself. A plan sometimes suggested is for the editor to send back to the writer any letter that he proposes to shorten, with a statement of the omissions to be made, and allow the writer to decide whether he wishes it to be published in this form. Objection has been raised to this plan on the ground of impracticability.

A newspaper is often enabled to add to its circulation and general financial strength by the more spectacular forms of editorial leadership or even of representing and enforcing public opinion. One is not justified in concluding even from the exclusively financial standpoint, however, that "a journalist can never succeed unless he is fathering popular or moral causes." [1] The recent history of such newspapers as *The Boston Transcript* and *The New York Times* proves the contrary. Even if financial strength can be most readily obtained in this way, it is too dearly purchased in case it interferes in any way with the function of the newspaper as a disseminator of objective facts.

Additional Readings

Villard, *Some Newspapers and Newspapermen.*
Davis, |*History of The New York Times,* pp. 81–116.
O'Brien, *The Story of The Sun,* pp. 304–312.
Heaton, *The Story of a Page.*
The .W. G. N., pp. 53–79.
Scott, *The Manchester Guardian: A Century of History.*
The Race Track Graft.   Pamphlet of *The Det, oit News.*
Lippmann, *Public Opinion,* pp. 358–365.
Leupp, *The Waning Power of the Press,* in Bleyer's *The Profession of Journalism,* pp. 30–51.

[1] Payne, *History of Journalism in the United States,* p. 326.

IX

Setting Professional Standards: Legal Measures

Whenever any scandal or even unpleasantness arises to ruffle the composure of the average American citizen as to government, civilization, or any such matter, he promptly fixes upon some individual or group of individuals whom he holds to be responsible, and asserts indignantly, "They ought to be put in jail." Or, in the event he realizes that there is no legal means whereby the culprits may be hurried to prison, he is prone to start his discussion, "There ought to be a law."

The faith of the American people in law is a problem for the psychologist rather than the journalist. That it exists as one of the facts of life in this country is not to be denied and must be faced by every public or quasi-public institution.

With this reliance of the public upon law it is not surprising that various laws have been proposed for the purpose of improving the press. Laws already in existence relate chiefly to libel, to obscene writing, and to the exclusion of certain types of advertising.[1] In general these, as interpreted by the courts, are fair to the newspaper and to the public. The principal exception is in the case of laws relating to obscene writing, which have been stretched in some instances to cover works of great literary significance,

[1] For a detailed discussion of laws governing the press, see Hales, *The Law of the Press.*

but this has affected magazine and book rather than newspaper publishers. Contempt proceedings against newspaper workers by sensitive judges have been unfair to the persons directly involved and have at the same time rendered it difficult for the press to perform its rightful function.

Further proposals for legal restriction of journalism are intended to compel newspapers to be accurate and fair by process of law. The most drastic of such suggestions is a plan devised to secure "compulsory veracity" in newspapers. The proposer of this plan is Edward Paul, wno advocates his plan in the following words:

"Compulsory veracity in the newspapers is no more an infringement on our democratic rights than compulsory purity in foods. In maintaining that a pure news act would be interfering with the 'freedom' of 'the press, the press leads us to infer that Democracy is more interested in a healthy body than in a healthy mind. A healthy mind is dangerous to Democracy only in so far as that Democracy is shielding a minority in the enjoyment of privileges it is not worthy of enjoying. A healthier public mind would send more of such men to Washington as are now making things disagreeable for the packers and for those interests that thrive on the intimate friendship of railroads. The people having gained the vote, the last resort of Privilege is to deceive the voter, as it did last November. We have almost reached the *caveat lector* stage of social evolution.

"It is of considerable importance that steps be taken before many years to bring about compulsory veracity in the newspapers. The pressure of economic circumstances may at any time make the masses aware of the fact that they cannot trust the organs for the dissemination of news. When they realize that, they are likely to inquire what sort of government it is which permits the overwhelming majority of the people to be tricked, while that majority, engaged in labor, has its back turned." [1]

To obtain absolute accuracy a law is proposed that "whoever shall publish in a newspaper or other periodical a statement wilfully misrepresenting the facts, or shall publish as facts statements known to them to be untrue or erroneous through gross carelessness, shall be guilty of a misdemeanor."

In addition to this law there would be reserved in every paper a column for a public literary defender "elected by the people, who could give due importance to buried news and supply the point of view frequently omitted."

"With this system in vogue," asserts the editor of *The Arbitrator*, the paper responsible for the plan, "it would be possible to retain the freedom of the press. For there should be no objection to the appearance of any startling opinions of the editor, provided the correct ideas were given equal prominence in the same paper. If the policy of the paper was to oppose the conscription of men or of wealth, every issue could also contain the reason why such opinions were untenable and objectionable in the eyes of the government official answerable to the people."

"Another way," this writer goes on to say, "would be to have all complaints against the press submitted to various local comissions appointed for the purpose of punishing by fine, suspension, etc., the periodical which printed lies, or of compelling the offender to print a denial in a prominent column. Such a commission would not only relieve the courts, but the term of office and personnel could be so arranged as to secure justice for the public."

While to the practicing journalist or the careful student

[1] This and the following quotations are from *The Arbitrator* for July, 1919 (Vol. 2, No. 2).

of journalism such suggestions are obviously absurd, they are gaining adherents constantly among those who do not understand newspaper conditions and who are prone to grasp at legal solutions of all problems. The proposed law making it a misdemeanor to misrepresent the facts might be employed effectively in cases where there is certainty of record but where reporters disregarded the facts and published invented material of their own. This rarely happens, however, except through carelessness. Reports of cases in court, of municipal records, of legislative and executive proceedings, are reasonably accurate as to facts, and a reporter who habitually misrepresented in such matters through carelessness or design would not be retained on any important paper.

On other matters there is frequently room for difference of opinion as to what facts really are until some plan is devised whereby they can be carefully and competently investigated. With widely conflicting testimony presented, as would certainly be the case, a jury would rarely, if ever, convict. The same would hold true in the event of a prosecution for carelessness. Any one who has had experience in court knows that juries are exceedingly ready to accept extenuating circumstances, and carelessness would readily be adopted as such in a newspaper case, as it is accepted today in many court proceedings.

Already laws exist in certain states to punish all persons who knowingly and wilfully transmit to any publication false and untrue statements of fact. Such a law exists in New York as Section 1353 of the Penal Code. It has been very seldom invoked. So innocuous has it been that many newspaper men do not know of its existence. When a similar law was passed by the Minnesota legislature recently, certain New York newspapers referred to it as if it were a new legal departure. A Massachusetts statute, passed in 1922, imposes fine or imprisonment for publishing false statements about candidates for public office.[1]

Granted that the proper means of establishing the veracity of the press is by law, it is obvious that the law proposed would be ineffectual. It would doubtless result in a number of prosecutions, mostly based on unimportant matters. These prosecutions would cover a short period of time after the law was adopted. Thereafter, the statute would become a dead letter, never invoked except for spite or in case of some flagrant violation, such as, however, is now covered by the laws punishing libel.

The suggestion of a public literary defender is still more absurd. Any one who has had experience as a newspaperman in dealing with public officials, from village councilmen to high officials of the United States, knows how little reliance can be placed upon their objectivity of view or their fairness in any matter in which their personal interests or the interests of their party are concerned. It may be urged that a public literary defender would represent the point of view of a majority of the people on contested questions. In this country, however, the number of contested issues is so great that no elected officials necessarily represent the point of view of a majority of the people upon these issues. These officials were elected by a combination of factors. Some voters cast their ballots on one issue, others on another issue. Furthermore, as has been previously pointed out, the public is not always—perhaps is never—seeking the complete objective facts, the dissemination of which is the highest function of the newspaper. The proposer of the office of literary defender naïvely admits this in referring to "the correct ideas." Manifestly,

[1] *General Laws of Massachusetts,* Chapter 55, Section 34a.

he belongs to that group of careless thinkers who consider
that correctness of opinion is to be established by majority vote.   In considering this point of view, one may well
reflect on what support the ideas of Socrates, of Galileo,
of Darwin, to take but a few examples, had from the majority opinion of their times.

A still more drastic legal provision is suggested by W. T.
Colyer,[1] who advocates that every paper should be compelled to devote at least half a column in every issue to
answering questions about its stockholders, employees, or
contributors.   He would make a requirement also that
every paper print in each issue a list of the letters submitted for publication but not intended to be published,
with a summary of the letters.   It is evident, of course, that
such proposals as Mr. Colyer's tend simply to confuse the
issue of accuracy by introducing the question of personal
bias on the part of editors or owners of the paper and by
representing the newspaper to be a public forum, which,
under the most widely social interpretation of its function,
it is not.   There is no obligation upon a newspaper to publish a letter which it receives, any more than there is an
obligation upon the owner or lessee of a hall to open the
platform for a reply to an appointed speaker.   There
is, of course, an obligation to correct errors of fact
when brought to the newspaper's notice by letter or otherwise.

Upton Sinclair naturally urges law for the government
of newspapers.   He proposes in *The Brass Check*[2] a law
providing that newspapers shall not publish an interview
with any one that has not been O. K.'d or concerning which
they have not the permission of the person interviewed to

[1] *Obligatory Answers,* in *The Arbitrator,* Vol. 2, No. 2, pp. 12–13.
[2] P. 404.

publish it without an O. K.   In point of fact certain newspapers make this requirement in the case of important matters.   In not a few cases persons who know they will be
interviewed on a matter prepare statements to be submitted
to the newspapers to express their views.   The Kansas
Newspaper Code of Ethics, adopted in 1910, advocated the
same proceeding that Mr. Sinclair advises.[1]

Generally speaking, the rule which is thus urged would
be impracticable because of limits of time in modern newspaper work.   Suppose a reporter interviews a man in the
Bronx in New York, then goes downtown to write his story
or telephone it to the office to be written.   In either event
the sending of a messenger from downtown New York to
the Bronx to obtain an O. K. on the interview would cause
editions to be missed.   Moreover, it would result in heavy
expenditures of money which the importance of the matter
would usually not justify.   In some cases, for example,
criminal matters, disappearance of the person interviewed
would make an O. K. impossible.

Furthermore, the requirement of an O. K. on interviews
would cause many written interviews, perfectly correct,
to be destroyed and others to be altered, because upon reading them the person interviewed would feel that what appeared in black and white, while perfectly true, was contrary to his private interests.   While undoubtedly interviews are sometimes faked or partly faked, every newspaper
man knows that a considerable proportion of those concerning which complaint is made represent the actual statements
of the persons interviewed.   An individual denies the interview merely because upon its publication he has felt it
to be unpopular or contrary to his own interests.   Certain
high officials have been notorious among newspaper re-

[1] See Appendix A, p. 206.

porters for denying interviews concerning which there was no question.

Mr. Sinclair also suggests "a law providing that when any newspaper has made any false statement concerning an individual and has had its attention called to the falsity of this statement, it shall publish a correction of the statement in the next edition of the publication and in the same place and with the same prominence given to the false statement." [1]

The French practice [2] with reference to corrections of errors and answers to attacks in newspapers is of interest here. The French law provides that when the official actions of public officers have been incorrectly reported or distorted, a newspaper is required to publish on the first page an answer of not more than twice the length of the injurious article. This answer must appear in the first issue following notification by the interested party. In case the answer is more than twice as long as the original, the newspaper may charge for the excess at the rate provided for legal notices.

With reference to private individuals named or designated in an untruthful news story, a newspaper must publish within three days after receiving it an answer twice as long as the original article. The answer must appear in the same place in the paper where the original article was published, and must be printed in the same type.

In practice, the law is seldom invoked, as newspapers regularly publish the answers sent to them without waiting for any form of legal notice.

---

[1] *The Brass Check*, p. 405.
[2] The writer is indebted to Professor P. de Bacourt of Columbia University for authoritative data on the French law and practice

Another law advocated by Upton Sinclair is one putting the distribution of news to American newspapers under public control. Mr. Sinclair, who believes the Associated Press to be a monopoly, desires that any one who wishes to publish a newspaper in any American city or town may receive the Associated Press service without any formality whatever except the filing of an application and the payment of a fee to cover the cost of the service.[1] In view of the fact that Mr. Sinclair believes the public opinion of America to be "poisoned at the source"[2] by this organization, it would seem anomalous that he should wish to extend its service. Laws of the sort advocated by Mr. Sinclair already exist in Kansas and Kentucky but have never been enforced, the handling of news being an interstate matter. Newspaper men, of course, know that the Associated Press is not a monopoly, the United Press and the International News Service being vigorous general competitors, and several other services being competitors in limited fields.

None of the foregoing suggestions represents the serious thought of any one practically experienced in journalism. The only proposed law which does represent the point of view of the professional journalist to any extent is the suggestion of a state board of journalism which should issue and revoke licenses to practice the profession of journalism. Such a law would be intended to introduce into the journalistic profession standards similar to those now existing in the legal and medical professions. One of the earliest suggestions of this character was made by Barratt O'Hara, a practicing newspaper man, formerly lieutenant governor of Illinois. Mr. O'Hara's plan, proposed in 1913, con-

[1] *The Brass Check,* p. 406.
[2] *The Brass Check,* pp. 362–376.

tained the following provisions, according to the author's own statement:

"A license should issue:

"1. When the applicant had reached legal age;

"2. Completed the equivalent of a high school education.

"3. Studied two years in a recognized college of journalism, or passed the same period of time in a newspaper office as an apprentice reporter;

"4. Furnished the Board with positive proof of good moral character; and

"5. Successfully passed an examination, in writing, conducted by the State Board at regular intervals.

"Adequate provision was made for the beginner, who might receive, on application to the Board and proof of good moral character and an education equivalent to that of the ordinary high school, a certificate as an Apprentice Reporter. As such he might perform the usual work of a cub reporter, but would be disqualified from passing final judgment on his own and other persons' copy. That is, he might write the items, but the same would be read and possibly revised by a licensed journalist before reaching the printer. Two years of such training and restriction, with the natural looking forward to the examinations ahead and the constant preparing for them, could scarcely fail to bring out the very best newspaper qualities in the young aspirant. Or the same period might be spent with equal profit in an approved and practicable school of journalism.

"A license, on the other hand, should be revoked:

"1. Automatically, on the practitioner's conviction of a felony; or

"2. After due filing of charges and trial by a jury of his fellow practitioners, for willful misrepresentation, malicious writing of scandal, acceptance of money or other prize tendered as bribe for the deliberate and unjustified coloring of news items,

---

[1] Thorpe, *The Coming Newspaper*, pp. 154–156.

or other conduct unprofessional, reprehensible, and dishonest." [1]

A somewhat similar bill was proposed in the Oklahoma legislature in 1923. It was strongly opposed by the newspapers of the state generally, which believed that it was inspired by a spirit of revenge rather than by a desire to improve journalistic conditions. The bill was defeated. The bill provided that the board should consist of the President of the State University, the Dean of the School of Journalism of the State University, and three members to be appointed by the governor. All of the appointed members were required to have had at least five years' active experience as newspapermen in Oklahoma. The revocation of licenses was made conditional on the following facts:

"(a) When it shall be ascertained that any applicant made any false statements or representations in procuring his license.

"(b) When any licensee is convicted of a crime against the laws of the State of Oklahoma involving moral turpitude.

"(c) When any licensee becomes an habitual drunkard.

"(d) When any licensee prints or causes to be printed, or permits the printing and publication of any story or news article about any citizen of this state or nation which is not true.

"(e) When any licensee prints, or causes to be printed, or permits the printing and publication of any news article, story or editorial, which either directly or by insinuation, falsely charges any citizen of this state or nation with an act which hurts the standing or reputation of such citizen in the community or state or nation, either in a business or social way.

"(f) When any licensee prints, causes to be printed or permits the printing and publication of any news item, editorial, or story which is immoral or degrading." [2]

[2] *Editor and Publisher*, March 17, 1923, p. 18.

Similar bills have been introduced in the legislature of Connecticut and possibly those of other states.

It is altogether probable that in time admission to the profession of journalism will be made conditional upon passing certain requirements. This will come, however, as the result of a demand from practicing journalists rather than from the outside. In accordance with the practice in every profession, any examining board would be composed of members of the profession. Until the ethical standards of the profession are more definitely established than they are today, the tendency of examinations and other acts of the board might conceivably be to preserve the present status of journalism and to hinder development of higher standards. A professional consciousness and the ethical and social implications flowing from this are necessary before any legal enactment can improve the status of journalism as a profession.

Additional Readings

Hale, *The Law of the Press.*

Angell, *The Press and the Organisation of Society,* pp. 76–89.

Sinclair, *The Brass Check,* pp. 403–407.

The Arbitrator, Vol. 2, No. 2, July, 1919.

O'Hara, *A State License for Newspaper Men,* in Thorpe's *1 he Coming Newspaper,* pp. 148–161.

Oklahoma Press Bill Is Doomed. Editor and Publisher, March 17, 1923, p. 18.

X

SETTING PROFESSIONAL STANDARDS: ORGANIZATIONS OF
JOURNALISTS

Among practicing journalists one of the most hopeful
signs for the general betterment of the profession is the
growth—though slow—of a professional spirit and of desire for a respect-commanding organization. Schools of
journalism, economic factors, and the realization that all
is not well with the press are influences in this direction.
Too many newspaper men, however, still regard their work
not as a profession, but merely as a job—and frequently
as a steppingstone to something else. They leave it for
positions ranging from publicity agent for a religious society
to salesman of blue-sky stock. This is not surprising, in
view of the low salaries paid in newspaper work and
the paradoxical situation which subjects the reporter to a
measure of contempt but at the same time places him in
direct contact with the influential in business, social, and
political life.

Other countries have made more progress than the United
States in organizing journalists and a glance at their methods
is enlightening. Particularly in England has such progress
been made that today practically every reporter and sub-
editor in the country now belongs to one of the three organizations of journalists.[1]

[1] The offices of these organizations, where application for information
concerning them may be made, are as follows:
Institute of Journalists, Tudor Street, London, E. C. 4.
National Union of Journalists, 180 Fleet Street, London, E. C. 4.

The oldest of these organizations is the Institute of Journalists, which was established by royal charter in 1889. The outgrowth of a smaller organization of progressive young men which was known as the National Society of Journalists and which was confined to provincial papers, it embodies the aspirations of idealistic youth and has made marked progress in many directions. It maintains an unemployment fund which provides benefits for thirteen weeks, a defense fund for the purpose of giving legal advice and dealing both in and outside the courts with literary and journalistic disputes in which the members become involved, a fund which assists the orphans of journalists, and another fund which provides insurance at low cost. An employment register free to all members is kept.

While the Institute has set no examinations or other special tests for prospective members, it expects eventually to adopt some such plan. This is provided for in the charter of the Institute, which also makes provision for various projects, some of which have not yet been undertaken but which are upheld as ideals before the members. The principal objects named in the charter are these:

"Devising measures for testing the qualifications of candidates for admission to professional membership in the Institute by examination in theory and in practice or by any other actual and practical tests.

"The promotion of whatever may tend to the elevation of the status and the improvement of the qualifications of all members of the journalistic profession.

"The ascertainment of the law and practice relating to all things connected with the journalistic profession and the ex-

Society of Women Journalists, Sentinel House, Southampton Row, London, W. C. 2.

ercise of supervision over its members when engaged in professional duties.

"The collection, collation, and publication of information of service or interest to members of the journalistic profession.

"Watching any legislation affecting the discharge by journalists of their professional duties and endeavoring to obtain amendments of the law affecting journalists, their duties, or interest.

"Acting as a means of communication between members, or others, seeking professional engagements and employers desirous of employing them.

"Promoting personal and friendly intercourse between members of the Institute; holding conferences and meetings for the discussion of professional affairs, interests, and duties; the compilation, constant revision, and publication of lists and registers of journalists and of records of events and proceedings of interest to journalists.

"The formation of a library or libraries for the use of members of the Institute.

"The encouragement, establishment, or development of a professional journal for journalists.

"The promotion, encouragement, or assistance of means for providing against the exigencies of age, sickness, death, and misfortune.

"The acquisition by the Institute of a hall or other permanent place of meeting and of other places of meeting.

"Securing the advancement of journalism in all its branches and obtaining for journalists, as such, formal and definite professional standing.

"The promotion by all reasonable means of the interests of journalists and journalism."

The Institute has subsidiary associations all over the British Empire. In the larger centers it has branches devoted to special types of journalism, such, for example, as trade journalism. In all its work it aims not only to lay down sound, ethical principles but to create opportunities for beneficial intercourse among journalists. It has been a potent force in developing professional consciousness among the newspaper men and women of England.

The National Union of Journalists, the other leading British organization of newspaper workers, was founded in 1906 as a trade union. It is affiliated with the Printing and Kindred Trades Federation of Great Britain. It has made rapid progress and in the spring of 1923 had a membership of 4,200, which it claims is more than three times that of any other organization of British journalists.

The National Union of Journalists consists exclusively of journalists dependent on their own work. It does not admit newspaper proprietors, directors, or managers, but the holding of shares in a newspaper company does not necessarily bar an otherwise eligible journalist from membership. It includes not only members of the staffs of newspapers but persons who in this country would be called free-lance writers. For example, H. G. Wells is a member of the Union.

The objects of the society, stated in its amended rules, are:

"1. To defend and promote the professional interests and status of its members with regard to salary, conditions of employment, tenure of office.

"2. The establishment of out-of-work, benevolent, and superannuation benefits.

"3. To deal with questions affecting the professional conduct of its members.

"4. To be an Approved Society within the meaning of the National Health Insurance Acts, and to transact business under the Acts, and to do all things required by the Acts, and by the

Ministry of Health for the purpose of so being an Approved Society and of transacting such business.

"5. To carry out the provisions of the Unemployed Insurance Act, 1920."

Marked attention has been given to the salary question. Salaries of newspaper workers in England had been shockingly low, due to a variety of causes, among which was the considerable number of persons of independent income in the profession. As the war raised prices, many journalists were faced with practical starvation. The Union, by this time strong enough to act, took steps to change these conditions, not only because of the economic necessity but because of the greater professional independence that is always secured to a man who is receives a living income.

The agreements made by the Union with newspaper proprietors in London and the provinces have increased salaries 100 to 200 per cent above the pre-war figures. Before the war some competent journalists were working in Fleet Street for as little as £3 a week. At present (1923) the minimum London rates range from £6 6s. for reporters on trade papers to £9 9s. on dailies and Sunday newspapers. On provincial weekly papers the minimum wage is £4 7s. 6d. and on provincial dailies £5 3s. In London fixed maximum working hours have also been established. These are 38½ hours a week for sub-editors—or copyreaders, as they would be called in the United States,—44 hours for reporters and photographers, and 48 hours for photo printers, who in England are classified as journalists. The Union has also obtained a three weeks' vacation each year for journalists in London.

Most of these accomplishments have been obtained by

trade union action with the support of the mechanical workers in the printing industry.

The Union has standing honorary counsel, who advises
on questions relating to journalists' rights and privileges.
The Union has fought cases arising out of radius agreements, copyright of written matter and photographs, wrongful dismissal due to insufficient notice, and payment of salary during sickness, and his recovered large sums of money
for members. Every case fought by the Union has been
won.

The Union maintains a register and also pays benefits
to unemployed members, £2 a week for the first thirteen
weeks and £1 a week for the next thirteen weeks. The
Union is an approved society under the National Health
Insurance acts of Great Britain. It is represented on the
London University Journalism Committee and on the Joint
Industry Council for the Newspaper Industry.

The other organization of working journalists in England is the Society of Women Journalists. Women are not
barred from the other societies, but a number of them
have organized in this society to deal with their own specific
problems.

In Australia, New Zealand, and South Africa journalists
are organized on the union basis. Indeed, the British National Union of Journalists has newspaper agreements with
the organizations in the colonies. In Australia and New
Zealand agreements between representatives of employing
newspapers and of working journalists are in effect under
the trade union laws of these colonies. These agreements
provide for hours, wages, including a minimum rate per
line for material furnished by correspondents, and other
details.

In the United States no organization exists comparable

to those in English-speaking countries abroad. There are a number of organizations of newspaper publishers, concerned to a large extent with business problems. There was recently organized the American Society of Newspaper Editors, which is concerned largely with ethical problems. It has adopted an admirable code of ethics. It is composed, nevertheless, exclusively of men holding high positions on newspapers, and only 124 of them,[1] although these papers possess special significance by reason of belonging to the metropolitan group. The various state press associations, which devote their attention to both business and professional problems, are likewise made up almost exclusively of newspaper proprietors. While it is highly desirable that there be organizations of this character, it is evident that they cannot represent the profession as a whole, since owners of newspapers are in a small minority. The professional interest of journalism must be supplied fundamentally by the mass of working journalists.

A number of national organizations of journalists have been attempted in this country. Most of them have made no marked headway. There are three reasons for this: (1) Lack of money to promote organization; (2) the individualism of newspaper workers; (3) hostility of newspaper publishers. Certain publishers, even of those professing to be liberal, have fought steadily all organization among their employees, preventing even the formation of such wholly social bodies as press clubs. Their reasons are obvious. On the other hand, opposition of that sort would be much less effectual were newspapermen themselves more ready to act collectively.

At present the field is open for a definite organization of newspaper workers. Among the most effective organiza-

[1] *Editor and Publisher,* April 28, 1923, p. 15.

tions now existing are Sigma Delta Chi and Theta Sigma Phi, respectively men's and women's professional journalism fraternities. These are but a few years old and their membership is relatively small, although it is rapidly growing in both numbers and influence. It includes, however, only college men and women, except such practicing journalists as may be admitted as associate members, and thus excludes the vast majority of actual newspaper workers in this country. Furthermore, election to membership is dependent on the same sort of ballot as in a lodge or social fraternity, and sometimes persons of marked ability and character fail of election. Steps in the direction of a more inclusive organization are under consideration by Sigma Delta Chi. There are in existence several other journalistic organizations such as the American Journalists' Association. Their membership is small.

Here and there American journalists have affiliated with the trade union movement.[1] In doing this they become members of the International Typographical Union, but an effort is now in progress to obtain from the American Federation of Labor recognition for a journalists' union.

The trade union plan of organization is looked upon with disfavor by most of them—and perhaps with some justice, since it suggests that journalism is a trade rather than a profession. On the other hand, there is nothing in the trade union idea that should essentially bar professional workers. The argument that the newspaper man should not affiliate with a labor organization because it will impair his impartiality overlooks the fact that newspaper men as such join Chambers of Commerce, Rotary Clubs, and similar

[1] For discussion of one such affiliation, see *News Writers' Local No. 1*, *The New Republic*, vol. 20, pp. 8–9.

organizations, without any protest on the part of those who look with horror on a trade union connection.

In Australia and New Zealand the same opposition arose when the movement began. Of the change in attitude, Dr. Walter Williams, who made a personal investigation, says:

"While the introduction of the wages-board or trade-union principle to journalism in these countries was opposed, sometimes with bitterness, by a majority of the employers and by a small minority of the employed, it has apparently resulted in considerable good. The objections urged against it in advance of its adoption were that it would lower the dignity of journalism, decrease the opportunities for the best journalists, level down salaries, and take from journalists the incentive which the professional rewards had given. These objections do not seem to have been well-founded. The employing publishers and chief editors of Australia are not unanimous in condemning the law. A few do condemn, but the great majority assert the law has not been in existence long enough to prove itself either good or bad, while a few express the opinion that it has resulted for the best interests of all parties. On the other hand, the working journalists, members of the Australian Journalists' Association, contend—and with show of truth—that wages have been increased, holidays have been granted, and, with a resulting improvement in the character of work done, the professional spirit has not diminished, while financial independence and permanence of employment have helped toward better writing and better newspapers." [1]

In England the situation was somewhat different. The trade union movement there is far in advance of that in the United States and has the active opposition of no important portion of the population. Moreover, the young

[1] *The World's Journalism,* p. 29.

graduates of the universities are more and more embracing the labor cause, many of them being active in the Labour Party. It is not surprising, therefore, that the National Union of Journalists should have received the commendation of Lord Northcliffe and other widely known publishers.

There is a further difference between the American and the British situation which makes the wage question there paramount. In England the editor is in control of his paper, regardless of whether he owns a share of stock or not. This is the age-old tradition. Consequently, the problem of the journalist in conflict with a publisher determined, through ignorance or dishonesty, to misrepresent the news is not a significant issue in England. There are signs of its development, however. The journalistic organizations already existing will possibly prevent its gaining a strong foothold.

In all probability the outlook for the distinctively professional organization of newspaper men and women is most favorable in the United States in the near future. It would perhaps follow to a considerable extent the plans of the British Institute of Journalists.

An organization embracing practically all working journalists could fix high standards of entrance into the profession, could establish a sound and workable code of ethics, and could insure adequate salaries in the profession. In all of these, of course, it would need public sympathy and cooperation. From the work of such an organization might develop eventually laws for examining and licensing journalists. There would also be a tendency toward the elimination of one of the most unfortunate features of the press, editorial control of newspapers by men who have had no professional training or experience in journalism and who consider journalism merely a business.

Additional Readings

Constitutions and rules of the Institute of Journalists, the National Union of Journalists, and the Society of Women Journalists.

Williams, *The World's Journalism, University of Missouri Bulletin,* Journalism Series 9, pp. 20–29.

Angell, *The Press and the Organisation of Society,* pp. 76–123.

Labour Research Department, *The Press,* pp. 35–43.

Sinclair, *The Brass Check,* pp. 415–428.

Bullen, *The English Substitute for the License Plan,* in Thorpe's *The Coming Newspaperman,* pp. 162–170.

News Writers' Union Local No. 1. The New Republic 20: 8–9.

American Bar Association, *Canons of Professional Ethics.*

American Medical Association, *Principles of Medical Ethics.*

XI

SETTING PROFESSIONAL STANDARDS: THE NEWSPAPER'S PART

Those who maintain that the press is essentially and consciously corrupt look for no improvement in the conditions of journalism from within the press itself. If they are sufficiently realistic in point of view to recognize the futility of legal measures as a corrective of evils in journalism, they are nevertheless prone to seek some other remedy, the impetus for which comes from outside the profession of journalism. Such an origin does not necessarily mean that a given proposal is unwise, but should lead the unprejudiced observer to regard it with caution, since it can hardly be presumed that any institution is wholly unwilling to be improved or unable to improve itself.

Aside from laws governing a privately owned press, the two suggestions most commonly made call respectively for endowed newspapers and for newspapers owned by the government, federal, state, or municipal.

Against both the endowed newspaper and the government-owned newspaper, one objection is commonly urged by practicing journalists; namely, that they would be too dull to appeal to the general public. Weight is given to this objection by a reading of government publications in general. Few of them possess interest except to the technical reader. *The Official Bulletin,* issued by the United States government during the recent war, was, although edited by a professional newspaperman, one of the dullest publications ever circulated. There are in this country no endowed newspapers, in the strict sense of the word, so that one cannot definitely pass judgment as to the probable interest of such publications. There are several magazines of opinion, however, which are practically endowed. However enjoyable and stimulating these may be to the intellectual reader, their small circulation proves their lack of appeal to the general public. If a publication is supported by the government or by private endowment, the staff does not feel strongly the necessity of interesting a large number of readers. While this might be beneficial in eliminating the ultra-sensational from a newspaper, it would at the same time reduce the value of the publication as a means of disseminating facts.

As to the endowed newspaper, another objection arises. Endowments are likely to be instituted for the purpose of advancing a particular cause rather than for the purpose merely of disseminating objective facts. Moreover, no matter how much care is taken to prevent it, there is a tendency for endowments to represent and perpetuate the mental attitude of the donors regardless of what the stated purpose of the endowment may be. This fact has been complained of time and again in the case of educational institutions, justly and unjustly; there is no reason to assume that the same complaints would not arise in the case of endowed newspapers. Once the complaint developed, whether well founded or not, much of the influence of the newspaper would be lost.

The government-owned newspaper is open to the objection that it would certainly be used for propaganda. Indeed, it seems astonishing that government newspapers should be seriously advocated by those who are familiar with the politician's attitude toward facts, and particularly by those who complain of current political conditions. The unreliability of purported facts furnished to newspapers by government officials has been emphasized again and again. The inability to reason from facts to conclusions and the practice of basing opinions purely on preconceived notions are apparent to any one who will read *The Congressional Record* or listen, as a newspaper reporter, to the press statements made by executive officials.

The theory that politicians would not take advantage of the opportunity of a government-owned newspaper to advance their own fortunes and those of their groups and parties, is untenable. The attempts of politicians to influence newspapers, privately owned, to misrepresent or suppress the facts, afford sufficient clue to what would happen were these same politicians in control of the financial support of the press. The method of the politician, even when he evidently considers he is acting for the best interests of the country, is illustrated by the following circular, issued when both Canada and the United States were engaged in the World War:

Circular No. C. P. C. 57a.

CONFIDENTIAL CIRCULAR FOR CANADIAN EDITORS
(Not for Publication.)

(1) Owing to the shortage of agricultural labourers in Canada, consequent upon the absence of such a large proportion of Canadian manhood on military service, and in view of the supreme importance of securing the highest possible production in natural products, the Government is making an effort to bring in from the United States to the Western Provinces as much farm labour as possible. Editors are asked

to suppress references to this particular matter, as it is feared that publicity may seriously interfere with the plan.

ERNEST J. CHAMBERS,
Chief Press Censor for Canada.

Office of the Chief Press Censor for Canada,
> Department of the Secretary of State,
>> Ottawa, January 19, 1918.

Where the private interests of the politician or his party, rather than apparently those of his country, are involved, he employs much less obvious, but for that reason more sinister, methods.

Furthermore, unless the government newspapers were given exclusive rights, they would fail of their purpose. The best journalists would still be found on privately owned papers, and the public would prefer the latter. This was found to be true when even semiofficial newspapers existed in Washington, in the first half of the nineteenth century.[1] To give exclusive rights to government newspapers would restore the abuses of seventeenth-century England, when the government endeavored to control all dissemination of news and all expression of opinion on public matters. At that time, of course, there was a clandestine press, just as there was in Belgium during the German occupation in 1914–1918, and eventually government control was done away with. The same thing would undoubtedly occur in the United States were the government to attempt to take over the press.

The one thing which can be done by the government to improve the press is to develop certainty of record on a greater number of matters, comparable to the certainty of record that now exists on court proceedings, the acts of legislative bodies, and some other events. Particularly

---

[1] See Payne, *History of Journalism in the United States*, pp. 238–239.

may this be wisely developed in social and economic problems. Mr. Lippmann's suggestion of intelligence bureaus, organized to supply facts but neither to render decisions nor to take action, presents a plan which, if efficiently carried out, would mean a decided advance for the newspaper in its capacity as a disseminator of objective facts. Such a system would have to be removed from direct political control, and it should, in turn, have no control over politics or over the press, but should be exclusively a fact-finding agency, as distinguished from a fact-disseminating, a policy-advocating, or an executive agency.[1]

So far as other governmental steps are concerned, they would in all probability be worse than useless. A government-controlled press would be essentially a propaganda press, whereas one of the chief accomplishments which newspapers of themselves can hope to make is freedom from propaganda.

The problem of propoganda is serious. Propaganda is practiced by every type of institution, from the patent medicine trade to the governments of important nations. Stimulated tremendously by the war, where its effectiveness was made manifest to the most skeptical, propaganda has obtained, by payment of large salaries, the services of exceedingly skillful thinkers and writers, commonly ex-journalists. Several years ago, there were 1,200 professional press agents and publicity experts in New York City alone. Today the number is doubtless much greater. A large newspaper will receive daily as much as 150,000 words from publicity bureaus of various sorts.

The purpose of the publicity agent, of course, is to get a favorable hearing for his side. He may adopt devious

---

[1] An outline of the plan, which should be read by every student of the press, is to be found in Mr. Lippmann's *Public Opinion*, pp. 369–410.

methods to accomplish his purpose. He may fake news; he may stage events for the purpose of "creating" news; he may "dress up" or even directly misrepresent news; he may endeavor to suppress news—all in order to produce a favorable impression of the cause that he is trying to advance. These are the abuses, embodying, in the person of a non-journalist, practically every charge that is made against the newspapers themselves. On the other hand, the publicity worker may be entirely honorable in his methods; he may merely present to the newspaper facts concerning his cause that otherwise might be overlooked. In this he does formally only what is done informally by every one who comes into contact with the press, and only in a limited sense is he a propagandist.

The danger of the propagandist to the press is partly in the abuses in which he often is involved, partly in the mere fact that he is a propagandist, and so skillful a propagandist that it is difficult for the journalist to obtain a fair view of situations into which professional propaganda has entered. Too, the presence of the press agent, or publicity expert, frequently keeps the investigating reporter from actual contact with the persons from whom he could obtain adequate information. Under such circumstances, reporting becomes a matter of accepting typed statements from the various persons connected with a news event, and these statements tend frequently to disguise rather than clarify the matters under consideration.

In behalf of the press agent, it must not be forgotten that in at least two ways newspapers have stimulated the professional development of propaganda. In the first place, reporters have so often misquoted speeches and otherwise misrepresented individuals that the latter in self-defense have turned to publicity bureaus as a means of placing exact statements in the hands of the newspapers. In the second place, reporters have failed to seek out news and have given most space to persons who would furnish them with typed copies of speeches, ready-prepared interviews, and similar material.

Although newspapers are in general fighting the growing tendency to propaganda, particularly where it clearly seeks to influence public opinion, they still display a disposition, when criticized, to throw the blame upon the persons or organizations involved in the news, and thus to invite further propaganda. For example, when the press was criticized for the slight space devoted to the convention of the National Education Association as compared with that devoted to the Dempsey-Gibbons fight,[1] the *Editor and Publisher* asserted of the association that "with a subject of interest to every home in the land it has not been able to put enough human interest into it to compete in a news sense, with a professional brawl in an out-of-the-way town on the plains of Montana."[2] The inference is plain: Education is important, but journalists cannot be expected to make the important interesting to the reader. The one who is involved in the news must put human interest into it. The easiest way, obviously, is through an expert press agent. This viewpoint is recognized by *The Christian Science Monitor*, which, in discussing the same matter, writes an editorial entitled *A Wider Field for the Press Agent*, in which it treats of "the indifference of the promoters" of education "to methods of awakening journalistic interest."[3]

That the function of the publicity agent, by whatever name called, will soon disappear under pressure of the

[1] Cf. supra, p. 113.
[2] Editorial, *Human Interest Stuff*, Editor and Publisher, July 14, 1923, p. 38.
[3] *The Christian Science Monitor*, July 24, 1923.

newspapers, is extremely unlikely, especially in view of their recognition in some cases, as just detailed, of his desirability. Until greater specialization, more marked investigative skill, and more pronounced readiness to go to trouble in obtaining news, are general among journalists, the publicity agent is likely to retain his place. What newspapers may practicably do toward freedom from propaganda is to accept the aid of the publicity agent only in supplying indubitable facts and in putting into popular language the technical details of specialized fields. Newspapers also may wisely refuse to accept any copy of any sort from any publicity agent who has once proved unethical in his conduct. The general practice of newspapers is in this direction. However blindly they may at times attack the problem, journalists realize essentially that the only press worth anything is a free press.

Aside from reducing the amount of propaganda, what, if anything, can the press as an institution do, toward raising the standards of journalism? The first step is to recognize that not all is well with the profession. This step has already been taken. While the universal tendency of the professional man to defend his profession against the laity still exists in journalism, the number of editorials in newspaper trade journals and even newspapers themselves about the faults of the press proves that the intelligent editor is not complacent. Too many publishers, who are not themselves editors, are complacent, but they are not likely to remain so indefinitely.

The second step is self-analysis. This is not an easy matter. The best plan, manifestly, would be an analysis of representative examples of the American press by a committee of whose objective-mindedness, fairness, and familiarity with journalistic practice there could be no doubt.

Such an investigation should cover various sections of the country and should include various types of newspapers, from the metropolitan daily to the country weekly. The few studies that have been made cover only large city dailies, whereas the vast majority of American newspapers and probably the weight of journalistic influence are found in the papers published in small towns. Furthermore, reports made by persons strongly opposed to the press or strongly in sympathy with it are useful in drawing public attention to conditions, but do not carry great evidential weight; indeed, in most cases they contain too little authenticated evidence to sustain any conclusions. An investigative project such as has been suggested would require a large endowment, but the results would more than justify it. The mere publication of the findings of the investigators would put the indubitable concrete facts about American journalism into the arena of public discussion, and this of itself would result in a speedy improvement. If a group of public-spirited publishers—or for that matter a group of any sort—would endow such an investigation, it would produce incalculable results for the betterment of journalism.

Until this is done, each newspaper must make its own analysis. A few papers are already doing so. *The Detroit News* employs an editorial secretary whose duties include investigation of the accuracy of statements in the paper. In 1913, Ralph Pulitzer established the Bureau of Accuracy and Fair Play of *The New York World*. The purpose, as stated by the founder, is "to promote accuracy and fair play, to correct carelessness, and to stamp out fakes and fakers." Every complaint made concerning an item in *The World* is investigated. If the complaint is justified, a correction is published, and the blame for the error is also fixed. The complainant is invariably informed of the results of the investigation. Faking or gross carelessness on the part of a reporter or correspondent subjects him to dismissal.[1] Some other newspapers follow similar practices on a less formal and elaborate scale. The better newspapers quite generally correct errors that are called to their attention, some in a "Beg Your Pardon" column established for the purpose, others in the regular news columns. This is a marked advance over the older practice of refusing to make corrections on the ground that they destroyed confidence in the press. There are still, it should be remarked in passing, newspapers which refuse to make corrections except of matters which they deem "important," and thus lead the public to utter disbelief in their integrity.

While it may seem at first glance that these methods constitute merely a negative method of self-analysis on the part of the newspapers, reflection will show that a publication could hardly initiate investigation of all the stories that it publishes, because of their vast number and the numerous lines of investigation that must be followed in tracing down the accuracy or inaccuracy of each. A newspaper might, however, initiate investigation of a certain number of stories each week, choosing those written by various members of the staff. A newspaper might also, still more practicably, publish in a prominent place in each issue an invitation to readers to complain of inaccuracies in any story. Undoubtedly many errors occur to which attention is never called but which would perhaps be brought to the notice of the paper were readers assured of the desire for their cooperation in the promotion of accuracy.

The third step that may be taken by the newspaper, the attempt to eliminate the faults which self-analysis shows,

[1] See Biennial Reports of the Bureau for details.

is illustrated in the practice of *The New York World*, heretofore mentioned. So far as the reporter is concerned, he will in most cases try to be accurate and fair if he knows that accuracy and fairness are wanted, and particularly if he knows that a penalty will be exacted for their violation. Many newspapers publish codes of ethics for the guidance of their staffs, which fact alone indicates a genuine interest in improving journalism. The same thing may be said of codes adopted by state press associations and similar bodies.[1] Unless the code is enforced, however, unless the reporter or other staff member, indeed, feels that there is behind it a vigorous moral purpose, it is likely to lead to few results. It is of course to be recognized that any code of ethics represents ideals rather than merely contemporary practice, but if the code is to be useful the practice must make an effort in the direction of actual conformity with the ideals set up.

So much for the newspapers as newspapers. Can the newspaper worker, reporter, copy-reader, or editorial writer, himself accomplish anything in the direction of maintenance of sound standards? He cannot, of course, do as an individual what a powerful organization of journalists could do. But he can do something. He can adopt a practical working code of ethics for himself. He can decide, for instance, that he will never intentionally write anything untrue or unfair, that he will never use any dishonorable means in securing news, that he will never violate a confidence, that he will never accept money or any other gratuity for writing or refraining from writing any item, that he will never knowingly give readers a false impression concerning any matter, however trivial. Having adopted a code, he can stand ready to be "fired" rather than violate it.

---

[1] See Appendix A for examples of codes of both types.

He is not, it is true, very likely to be "fired," for intentional, studied dishonesty on the part of newspapers, it has been pointed out, is not the chief reason for their deficiencies.

Such betterment of conditions as can be accomplished by the various individualistic means suggested reaches mainly, it is evident, the more casual deficiencies of the press—inaccuracy, general carelessness, so-called "harmless" faking, and the like. The underlying causes can be reached by no such application of palliatives. They will be eliminated slowly, chiefly by organization and educational agencies in coöperation with the press itself.

Additional Readings

Payne, *History of Journalism in the United States*, pp. 230–239.
Williams, *A History of British Journalism to the Foundation of the Gazette.*
Massart, *The Secret Press in Belgium.*
Lippmann, *Public Opinion*, pp. 369–410.
Sinclair, *The Brass Check*, pp. 408–414, 438–443.
Brown, *The Menace to Journalism. The North American Review*, 214: 610–618.
Brownell, *Publicity and its Ethics. The North American Review*, 215: 188–196.
Brown, *A Comment. The North American Review*, 215: 197–199.
Chafee, *Freedom of Speech*, pp. 1–228.
Blythe, *Pro Bono Publicity. The Saturday Evening Post*, August 4, 1923, pp. 20–21.
Biennial Reports of *The New York World's* Bureau of Accuracy and Fair Play.
Files of *The Official Bulletin.*

XII

SETTING PROFESSIONAL STANDARDS: EDUCATIONAL AGENCIES

The progress of society has always depended largely on education under the leadership of persons of creative intelligence. Improvement in journalism will come in the same way. Ignorance, inertia, and fear—psychological phenomena all of them—are, it has been observed, the principal causes for the deficiencies of American newspapers in respect to their primary function of presenting objective facts to the public. Psychological factors are eliminated, sublimated, or otherwise controlled, in the mass as in the individual, only by means of education. By the same means, the conscious factors that play a certain part in keeping the press from fulfilment of its functions may be done away with; education of the right type is one of the best guaranties against anti-social acts.

The education necessary for these purposes is not simply schooling. It is not the supplying of ready-made theories and conclusions to students. Persons who have had much schooling are often ignorant, lazy, and pathologically timid. At the same time, we must depend on the general school system plus such other aids as can be enlisted. The school system is established, it has public support—even if lukewarm at times,—and it is susceptible of practical improvement. What, then, may be done for the betterment of journalistic practice by the schools of the United States?

What may they accomplish toward the elimination of conscious anti-social tendencies in the press, and, more important, of ignorance, inertia, and fear as factors in journalism?

In discussions of education in relation to journalism, the school of journalism must occupy a significant place. There are twenty institutions in the United States offering degree curricula in journalism, while more than 200 other colleges and universities offer some instruction on the subject. The number of students now making professional preparation for journalism in institutions of higher learning is not less than 2,500, while the number of practicing journalists is estimated at under 60,000. The proportion of college students of journalism to practicing journalists is greater than was the proportion of college students of law and of medicine to practicing lawyers and physicians, respectively, forty years ago. The young men and women now studying journalism in schools designed for the purpose will be an important factor—perhaps the most important factor—in American newspaper work not many years hence.

The instruction, the purposes, and the ideals of schools of journalism thus become a matter of deep public concern. There are two distinct conceptions of the schools of journalism, and each has its supporters among the schools themselves. One conception is that the function of the school of journalism is to produce reporters who can write "good stories." Advocates of this conception are prone to argue publicly that newspapers want only reporters and that if the school can produce reporters they can learn in the newspaper office all else that they need to know about "the game." A school of this type emphasizes above everything else newspaper technique. This is the trade-school method, and it turns out graduates who have the competency which a trade school gives. They are facile, self-confident, and outwardly efficient. In their first year out of.school, they give good accounts of themselves as reporters go on American newspapers.

The school of this type is run frankly to furnish reporters for American newspapers—the same sort of reporters, with perhaps a little added polish, tact, and suavity, for the same sort of American newspapers that is current today. The school is commended by copy-readers, city editors, and even publishers for giving sound, practical teaching—"none of this theoretical stuff on rights and responsibilities and ethics." "By God!" such a publisher exclaims, "all the ethics a reporter needs is loyalty to his paper. I want men who'll be as loyal to this paper as they are to the flag." And from the trade school the publisher gets the men who will swear by his variant.

The other conception of the school of journalism is that journalism is a profession and that the school of journalism is a professional school. It admits that the school must give technical training in newspaper writing, but maintains that this technical training could be obtained in a very brief course and that the primary function of the school is rather to give the student such an intellectual and ethical training and background as will best enable him to serve the public through the press.

Like the trade school, the professional school of journalism aims to train reporters, for it realizes that capable, honest reporters are the foundation stone of a dependable press. But its conception of a reporter is not a man who can write "a good story." It is rather a trained investigator seeking the objective facts.

If such a school is even to approximate its practice to its

ideals, it must encourage men and women of the proper
natural qualifications to study for journalistic careers and
must discourage those who lack the necessary qualifications. Aside from integrity, intelligence and objective-
mindedness are the qualities most needed. Tact, ability to
meet people pleasantly, interest in humanity, and many
other qualities are desirable, but not of supreme importance.
Without intelligence, however, the work of a journalist is
essentially futile. He may go through various professional
motions, but he will never know what he is doing or why
he is doing it. Without objective-mindedness on the part
of journalists, the press will invariably fail to fulfill its
principal function. The sincerity of a reporter may be beyond question, but if his head is always full of opinions instead of facts he can do nothing but harm to his profession.

In a school maintaining professional ideals, there must
also be such a curriculum as will still further develop the
natural intelligence and objective-mindedness of prospective
journalists and will dispel the ignorance characteristic of
college students and graduates. This means the introduction of such special courses, dealing intelligently and freely
with current events, as often are not offered elsewhere in
the college or university. It requires the development of
realistic courses in politics, economics, and sociology, instead of the academic courses which deal only with the
theory and never with the actual workings of institutions.
It must supply the scientific basis for understanding the
vast technical developments of contemporary civilization.
It must furnish training in what constitutes evidence, in
order that the future reporter may not be misled by intentional or unintentional attempts to deceive him. In every
subject that it presents, such a school aims to develop in
the student complete intellectual honesty, the acceptance of

no doctrine because it is held by the herd, or because it is professed by the newspapers, or for any other reason than that after straightforward thinking he is convinced of its truth.

The professional school of journalism, moreover, shows an increasing tendency to encourage its students to specialize in specific phases of modern life—in international affairs, in commerce, in labor, in agriculture, in politics, and in other important fields—in order that in their newspaper work they may be prepared the better to serve civilization. The general public depends upon the newspapers for understanding of contemporary life. Contemporary life is complex, and no one person is qualified to deal with many phases of it. The old conception of the pretended omniscience of the journalist has disappeared, and more and more the public demands newspaper men and women who not only can write but know the fields about which they write.

The school of journalism which maintains these conceptions and standards has an uphill job, but not an impossible one. For most of the schools of journalism are making definite progress along precisely these lines. But they are making progress against odds.

In the first place, they have sometimes the opposition of newspaper publishers. There is developing in the United States a theory that certain institutions of learning or certain departments within them exist primarily for the selfish benefit of those to whose vocations their work is most closely related. One tries to serve the physician, another the business man, another the engineer, another the farmer. These men regard the schools or departments as in a measure their property. The newspaper publisher frequently looks upon the school of journalism as designed primarily to serve him, to prepare men to do what he wants them to do on his newspaper. The strictly professional school of journalism, on the contrary, takes the position that the purpose of every educational institution is to serve all humanity by means of the truth. Specifically with reference to journalism, it holds that the young man or woman going out to work on a paper is not primarily a servant of that paper, but rather a servant of humanity. It maintains that while the man who serves his publisher at the expense of humanity may win his publisher's praise, he nevertheless is a traitor to civilization. The professional school of journalism wants the suggestions and advice of newspaper men, but it wants them with the understanding that the interests of humanity and not the preservation of the *status quo* in journalism are paramount.

Not only does the professional school of journalism run counter sometimes to the wishes of newspaper men; it also must resist the pressure, brought to bear on all educational institutions by the rich, by politicians, by clergymen, and by other groups of the population, to accept without investigation the dogmas of the herd. The public, which the school is striving to serve, is often ungrateful, especially where the service involves the discovery and presentation of unwelcome truth.

Every citizen who is interested in the fulfillment by newspapers of their primary function of presenting the objective facts, may wisely interest himself in the professional school of journalism; in its battle with ignorance and fear it offers genuine hope for the future. The trade school of journalism, on the other hand, deserves no support, except, perhaps, from newspapers that want to employ its graduates.

Along with the trade school of journalism should be abolished all high school courses professing to teach journalism as a vocation. A resolution opposing such courses was unanimously adopted by the National Council of Teachers of English in 1920, and since such courses are commonly offered in connection with the English work, only the fatuity of school administrators or the pressure of newspapers seeking cheap and impressionable employees is likely to cause the retention of such courses. They offer merely cheap journalistic technique, giving the student none of the intellectual and ethical preparation necessary to a proper professional career. Their very existence makes it practicable for a newspaper proprietor whose employees leave him because of his dishonest or unfair practices, to fill their places with boys and girls who have neither the intelligence nor the courage to resist domination. Vocational high school courses in journalism are, of course, to be carefully distinguished from those courses in which training in news writing is used merely as a means of motivating and making practical the instruction in English composition.

In all colleges, regardless of what conceptions are maintained in the teaching of journalism, a gain will be made for democratic civilization, in the writer's estimation, if faculty censorship of news contained in student papers or sent to other newspapers by student correspondents is abolished. The writer makes this statement advisedly, after careful thought, after some years of experience in both journalism and teaching, and with a considerable knowledge of journalistic conditions in American colleges. Collegiate censorship, where it exists, is not a censorship for eliminating inaccurate or libelous matter, for in rigidly censored college papers one may find ridiculous inaccuracies and statements which would justify submission to a jury in a suit for libel. The censorship exists primarily for the purpose of keeping from the public, within or without the college, such facts as the authorities of the institution feel that the public ought not to know. It is, in short, a convenient device for suppressing the truth. The recently retired president of one institution with which the writer is acquainted permitted students of the college to hold dances, although the Church whose members largely support the institution is opposed to dancing. The president, a clergyman of this Church, forbade the college newspaper to mention dancing, stipulating that in its columns dances must always be referred to by other names. In discussing this matter with a student editor he said frankly that supporters of the college would cause much trouble if he did not conceal the fact that he permitted dancing. One need not sympathize with the prejudices of the college supporters in order to recognize the ethical character of the example set by the college president.

The argument in favor of censorship in colleges is twofold: First, that students lack judgment; second, that suppression of the facts is often for the "higher good." The first argument is perfectly true,—but students learn judgment only by exercising it, and any editor, student or other, is sobered by responsibility for everything he does. Moreover, the ill effects of censorship far outweigh the difficulties and embarrassments that may result from the unsound judgment of students. No university or college can honorably make use of the second argument. There is no higher good than the truth, to the discovery and dissemination of which all honest education is dedicated.

The effect of such casuistry as has just been discussed is to impress students with the conviction that truth is not the highest good and may properly be concealed or misrepresented in order to gain ends which are thought desirable. The principle back of this is the same physical fear and distrust of the people which, as has been observed, actuate newspaper men in deciding that certain facts are not good for the public to know. Not only students directly concerned with the college publications, but all the students who know of the system, are affected. They go into journalism active supporters of news suppression and misrepresentation, and into other walks of life passive apologists for it. Unconsciously, through precept and example, they have been made fundamental disbelievers in government by the people, in that they uphold the principle of withholding from the people that which alone makes the people capable of government.

While considering education, one must not overlook the fact that the psychological factors which in large measure account for the deficiencies of the American newspaper are not to be found exclusively in journalism. On the contrary, they permeate American life. Consequently, a program of education for the improvement of the press must not stop with the education of future journalists or even with college students in general. A more thorough-going process must be devised.

The newspapers are read more extensively than any other publication in the United States. Is it not an anomaly that in most schools—even most high schools and colleges—the newspaper is not mentioned from September to June? Would one not be astounded if the judiciary or the legislative branch of the government were not mentioned in the schools? Yet for knowledge of the doings of their courts and of their legislative bodies the people must depend on the newspapers. For the very information which enables them to decide whom they want for their elected judges and whom for their representatives, they must depend on the newspapers. From the time when the child is old enough to be able to read until he is graduated from the university, the newspaper should be brought to his attention and studied as a social phenomenon. He should be made to understand that without a truthful press a successful popular government is impossible and that without the cooperation of the public a truthful press is impossible. He should be brought to see that any attempt by any individual or group of individuals to cause a newspaper to suppress, falsify, color, or misrepresent in any manner any fact is a blow at the truthfulness of the press and consequently at popular government. Let the youth once be brought to esteem as a traitor to popular government any man or woman who attempts to influence the press to depart from its obligation to print the facts, and such treason to popular government will become rare.

If general education is to aid in making the press more useful in a democratic society, it must also recognize and make clear the fact which Mr. Lippmann points out, that every human being is surrounded by two environments, one of them real, the other composed of "the pictures in our heads" which we assume to be the real environment and upon which we act. While it is desirable to remove as far as possible the contradictions between these two environments, it is not practicable altogether to introduce into our minds a true and complete picture of the real environment. In a complex civilization there must be certain stereotypes, certain generalities; not everything can be seen in detail. The schools must recognize this situation, and must emphasize the necessity of humility about one's beliefs, ability to recognize stereotypes as such, and readiness to modify or discard them as may be necessary to conform to dis-covered facts.[1]

Education in this direction will tend toward elimination of fear as a characteristic of the public mind and conse-quently of the press. In particular, the unconscious fear of the herd will tend to disappear once it is clearly under-stood that opinion is merely opinion and that no belief, how-ever universal, is immune from evidential examination. Likewise, fear of facts in any phase of life will be seen to be ridiculous when they are used, not to bolster up precon-ceived opinions, but to test all opinions and to arrive at new conclusions.

The process of attaining this condition of affairs may not be a short one; it will doubtless seem unnecessarily long to those who believe that righteousness will immediately triumph if but given the aid of a few new laws or at most a new social and economic system. Yet, when one con-siders the progress made in the natural sciences in a rela-tively brief time against great odds, one may well wonder if perchance the accomplishment of similar ends in journalism may not come sooner than is commonly expected. What-ever the rate at which results may be attained, it is certain that there is no more significant field for effort. Every effort toward better journalism forms a part of the struggle against ignorance, inertia, and fear. Conversely, every step which is taken to release the American people from bondage to these forces of hopelessness is a step toward releasing also the American newspaper. For ignorance, inertia, and fear are the unchanging foes of the one thing which makes the newspaper useful, and genuine popular government pos-sible—truth.

[1]For a detailed discussion of this problem, see Mr. Lippmann's *Public Opinion*, pp. 3–32, 79–156.

Additional Readings

Proceedings of the American Association of Teachers of Journalism, 1921 and 1922.

Hornaday, *Education for Journalism in the United States,* in Williams's *The Press Congress of the World in Hawaii,* pp. 115–155.

Lee, *Instruction in Journalism in Institutions of Higher Education.*

Harrington, *Journalism as a Part of College. The Forum* 67 : 476–484.

Harger, *Journalism as a Career,* in Bleyer's *The Profession of Journalism,* pp. 264–277.

Williams, *The Newspaperman,* pp. 114–144.

Lippmann, *Liberty and the News,* pp. 69–104.

Lippmann, *Public Opinion,* pp. 3–32, 79–156.

APPENDIX A
CODES OF ETHICS AND RULES ADOPTED BY ORGANIZATIONS OF JOURNALISTS AND BY NEWSPAPERS

CODES OF ETHICS ADOPTED BY ORGANIZATIONS OF JOURNALISTS

CANONS OF JOURNALISM [1]

The primary function of newspapers is to communicate to the human race what its members do, feel, and think. Journalism, therefore, demands of its practitioners the widest range of intelligence, of knowledge, and of experience, as well as natural and trained powers of observation and reasoning. To its opportunities as a chronicle are indissolubly linked its obligations as teacher and interpreter.

To the end of finding some means of codifying sound practice and just aspirations of American journalism these canons are set forth:

I

Responsibility. The right of a newspaper to attract and hold readers is restricted by nothing but considerations of public welfare. The use a newspaper makes of the share of public attention it gains serves to determine its sense of responsibility, which it shares with every member of its staff. A journalist who uses his power for any selfish or otherwise unworthy purpose is faithless to a high trust.

II

Freedom of the Press. Freedom of the press is to be guarded as a vital right of mankind. It is the unquestion-

[1] Written by the Committee on Ethics (Harry J. Wright, Chairman), American Society of Newspaper Editors, and adopted by the Society in 1923.

able right to discuss whatever is not explicitly forbidden by law, including the wisdom of any restrictive statute.

III

Independence. Freedom from all obligations except that of fidelity to the public interest is vital.

1. Promotion of any private interest contrary to the general welfare, for whatever reason, is not compatible with honest journalism. So-called news communications from private sources should not be published without public notice of their source or else substantiation of their claims to value as news, both in form and substance.

2. Partisanship in editorial comment which knowingly departs from the truth, does violence to the best spirit of American journalism; in the news columns it is subversive of a fundamental principle of the profession.

IV

Sincerity, Truthfulness, Accuracy. Good faith with the reader is the foundation of all journalism worthy of the name.

1. By every consideration of good faith a newspaper is constrained to be truthful. It is not to be excused for lack of thoroughness or accuracy within its control or failure to obtain command of these essential qualities.

2. Headlines should be fully warranted by the contents of the articles which they surmount.

V

Impartiality. Sound practice makes clear distinction between news reports and expressions of opinion. News reports should be free from opinion or bias of any kind.

1. This rule does not apply to so-called special articles

unmistakably devoted to advocacy or characterized by a signature authorizing the writer's own conclusions and interpretations.

VI

Fair Play. A newspaper should not publish unofficial charges affecting reputation or moral character without opportunity given to the accused to be heard; right practice demands the giving of such opportunity in all cases of serious accusation outside judicial proceedings.

1. A newspaper should not invade private rights or feelings without sure warrant of public right as distinguished from public curiosity.

2. It is the privilege, as it is the duty, of a newspaper to make prompt and complete correction of its own serious mistakes of fact or opinion, whatever their origin.

VII

Decency. A newspaper cannot escape conviction of insincerity if while professing high moral purpose it supplies incentives to base conduct, such as are to be found in details of crime and vice, publication of which is not demonstrably for the public good. Lacking authority to enforce its canons, the journalism here represented can but express the hope that deliberate pandering to vicious instincts will encounter effective public disapproval or yield to the influence of a preponderant professional condemnation.

THE WASHINGTON CODE OF ETHICS [1]

I Will Be
Truthful in News
Truthful in Editorials
Truthful in Advertising
True to all My Obligations
Honest with My Competitors
True to the Ideals of Journalism
Mindful of the Value of Sincerity
Faithful to Community, State, Nation
Firm in Publication of Clean News
Honorable in all of My Dealings
Thorough in all of My Studies
Unselfish in all My Services
Faithful to all My Friends
Fair to all My Critics

[1] Written by Chapin D. Foster and others and adopted by the Washington State Press Association in 1923.

THE OREGON CODE OF ETHICS FOR JOURNALISM [1]

"Not only all arts and sciences but all actions directed by choice aim at some good."

> —Aristotle, Nicomachean Ethics, I. 1.

PREAMBLE

We believe in the teaching of the great ethicists that a general state of happiness and well-being is attainable throughout the world; and that this state is the chief end-in-view of society.

We recognize an instinct in every good man that his utterances and his deeds should make a reasonable and continuous contribution toward this ultimate state, in the possibility of which we reiterate our belief, however remote it may now seem.

We believe that men collectively should also follow the principles of practice that guide the ethical individual. For whatever purpose men are associated, we believe they should endeavor to make the reasonable and continuous contribution that distinguishes the ethical man. And all the agencies and instrumentalities employed by men, singly or collectively, should be based upon the best ethical practice of the time, so that the end-in-view of society may thereby be hastened.

[1] Written by Dean Colin V. Dyment, University of Oregon, and adopted by the Oregon State Editorial Association in 1922.

Of all these agencies the printed word is most widely diffused and most powerful. The printed word is the single instrument of the profession we represent, and the extent to which it is shaping the thoughts and the conduct of peoples is measureless. We therefore pronounce the ethical responsibility of journalism the greatest of the professional responsibilities, and we desire to accept our responsibility, now and hereafter, to the utmost extent that is right and reasonable in our respective circumstances.

Accordingly we adopt for our guidance the following code, which shall be known as the Oregon Code of Ethics for Journalism.

I. SINCERITY; TRUTH

The foundation of ethical journalism is sincerity. The sincere journalist will be honest alike in his purposes and in his writings. To the best of his capacity to ascertain truth, he will always be truthful. It is his attitude toward truth that distinguishes the ethical from the unethical writer. It is naturally not possible that all writing can be without error; but it can always be without deliberate error. There is no place in journalism for the dissembler; the distorter; the prevaricator; the suppressor; or the dishonest thinker.

The first section of this code therefore provides that we shall be continuously sincere in professional practice; and sincerity as journalists means, for example, that:

1. We will put accuracy above all other considerations in the written word, whether editorial, advertisement, article, or news story.

2. We will interpret accuracy not merely as the absence of actual misstatement, but as the presence of whatever

is necessary to prevent the reader from making a false deduction.

3. In an ethical attitude toward truth, we will be open at all times to conviction, for the sincere journalist, while fearless and firm, will never be stubborn; therefore we will never decline to hear and consider new evidence.

4. If new evidence forces a change of opinion, we will be as free in the acknowledgment of the new opinion as in the utterance of the old.

5. We will promote a similar attitude in others toward truth, not asking or permitting employees to write things which as sincere journalists we would not ourselves write.

II. Care; Competency; Thoroughness

Inaccuracy in journalism is commonly due more to lack of mental equipment than to wilfulness of attitude. The ill-equipped man cannot be more competent as a journalist than he can as a doctor or engineer. Given an ethical attitude, the contribution that each journalist makes to his community and to society is nearly in ratio to his competency. We regard journalism as a precise and a learned profession, and it is therefore the second part of this code that:

6. By study and inquiry and observation, we will constantly aim to improve ourselves, so that our writings may be more authentic, and of greater perspective, and more conducive to the social good.

7. We will consider it an essential in those we employ that they not merely be of ethical attitude, but reasonably equipped to carry out their ideals.

8. We will make care our devotion in the preparation of statements of fact and in the utterance of opinion.

9. We will advocate in our respective communities the same thoroughness, sound preparation, and pride of craft, that we desire in ourselves, our employees, and our associates.

10. We are accordingly the active enemies of superficiality and pretense.

III. JUSTICE; MERCY; KINDLINESS

Liberty of the press is, by constitution, statute, and custom, greater in the United States than anywhere else in the world. This liberty exists for our press so that the liberty of the whole people may thereby be guarded. It so happens that at times the liberty of the press is exercised as license to infringe upon the rights of groups and of individuals: because custom and law have brought about certain immunities, it happens that in haste or zeal or malice or indifference, persons are unjustly dealt by. Yet the freedom of the press should at all times be exercised as the makers of the constitution, and the people themselves through their tolerance, have intended it. The reputations of men and women are sacred in nature and not to be torn down lightly. We therefore pronounce it appropriate to include in this code that:

11. We will not make "privileged utterance" a cloak for unjust attack, or spiteful venting, or carelessness in investigation, in the cases of parties or persons.

12. We will aim to protect, within reason, the rights of individuals mentioned in public documents, regardless of the effect on "good stories" or upon editorial policy.

13. We will deal by all persons alike so far as is humanly possible, not varying from the procedure of any part of this code because of the wealth, influence, or personal situa-

tion of the persons concerned, except as hereinafter provided.

14. It shall be one of our canons that mercy and kindliness are legitimate considerations in any place of journalism; and that if the public or social interest seems to be best conserved by suppression, we may suppress; but the motive in such instances must always be the public or social interest, and not the personal or commercial interest.

15. We will try so to conduct our publication, or to direct our writing, that justice, kindliness, and mercy will characterize our work.

IV.   MODERATION;   CONSERVATISM;   PROPORTION

Since the public takes from the journalist so great a proportion of the evidence upon which it forms its opinions, obviously that evidence should be of high type. The writer who makes his appeal to the passions rather than to the intellect is too often invalid as a purveyor of evidence because his facts are out of perspective. By improper emphasis, by skillful arrangement, or by devices of typography or rhetoric, he causes the formation in the reader's mind of unsound opinion. This practice is quite as improper as and frequently is more harmful than actual prevarication. Through this code we desire to take a position against so-called sensational practice by acceptance of the following canons:

16. We will endeavor to avoid the injustice that springs from hasty conclusion in editorial or reportorial or interpretative practice.

17. We will not overplay news or editorial for the sake of effect when such procedure may lead to false deductions in readers' minds.

18. We will regard accuracy and completeness as more vital than our being the first to print.

19. We will try to observe due proportion in the display of news to the end that inconsequential matter may not seem to take precedence in social importance over news of public significance.

20. We will in all respects in our writing and publishing endeavor to observe moderation and steadiness.

21. Recognizing that the kaleidoscopic changes in news tend to keep the public processes of mind at a superficial level, we will try to maintain a news and an editorial policy that will be less ephemeral in its influence upon social thought.

V.   PARTISANSHIP; PROPAGANDA

We believe that the public has confidence in the printed word of journalism in proportion as it is able to believe in the competency of journalists and have trust in their motives.   Lack of trust in our motives may arise from the suspicion that we shape our writings to suit non-social interests, or that we open our columns to propaganda, or both. Accordingly we adopt the following professional canons:

22. We will resist outside control in every phase of our practice, believing that the best interests of society require intellectual freedom in journalism.

23. We will rise above party and other partisanship in writing and publishing, supporting parties and issues only so far as we sincerely believe them to be in the public interest.

24. We will not permit, unless in exceptional cases, the publishing of news and editorial matter not prepared by ourselves or our staffs, believing that original matter is the best answer to the peril of propaganda.

VI. PUBLIC SERVICE AND SOCIAL POLICY

We dispute the maxim sometimes heard that a newspaper should follow its constituency in public morals and policy rather than try to lead it. We do not expect to be so far ahead of our time that our policies will be impractical; but we do desire to be abreast of the best thought of the time, and if possible to be its guide. It is not true that a newspaper should be only as advanced in its ethical atmosphere as it conceives the average of its readers to be. No man who is not in ethical advance of the average of the community should be in the profession of journalism. We declare therefore as follows:

25. We will keep our writings and our publications free from unrefinement, except so far as we may sincerely believe publication of sordid details to be for the social good.

26. We will consider all that we write or publish for public consumption in the light of its effect upon social policy, refraining from writing or from publishing if we believe our material to be socially detrimental.

27. We will regard our privilege of writing for publication or publishing for public consumption as an enterprise that is social as well as commercial in character, and therefore will at all times have an eye against doing anything counter to social interest.

28. We believe it an essential part of this policy that we shall not be respecters of persons.

VII. ADVERTISING AND CIRCULATION

We repudiate the principle of "letting the buyer beware." We cannot agree to guarantee advertising, but we assume a definite attitude toward the advertising that we write, solicit, or print. We believe that the same canons of truth and justice should apply in advertising and circulation as we are adopting for news and editorial matter. We therefore agree to the following business principles:

29. We will coöperate with those social interests whose business it is to raise the ethical standard of advertising.

30. We will discourage and bar from our columns advertising which in our belief is intended to deceive the reader in his estimate of what is advertised. (This clause is intended to cover the many phases of fraud, and unfair competition, and the advertising of articles that seem likely to be harmful to the purchaser's morals or health.)

31. We will not advertise our own newspaper or its circulation boastfully, or otherwise, in terms not in harmony with the clauses of this code of ethics. (This is intended to cover misleading statements to the public or to advertisers as to the whole number of copies printed, number of paid-up subscribers, number of street sales, and percentage of local circulation.)

32. We will not make our printing facilities available for the production of advertising which we believe to be socially harmful or fraudulent in its intent.

To the foregoing code we subscribe heartily as a part of our duty to society and of our belief that the salvation of the world can come only through the acceptance and practice by the people of the world of a sound and practical ethical philosophy.

SOUTH DAKOTA CODE OF ETHICS [1]

We of the profession of journalism, especially of that department which has to do with the publication of newspapers, deem it fitting that a code of ethics be set down to embody those ideals of service and that sense of propriety and honor which should imbue the motives and guide the actions of all who enter upon this profession.

This code of ethics is founded upon the basic principle of truth and justice. It is to be kept as nearly inviolate as is possible in the alignment of human aspirations with the golden rule of conduct, "Whatsoever ye would that they do unto you, do ye so unto them."

SERVICE

The profession of journalism occupies the place of an essential service in its relations to the public. Its implied contract with the reader invites trust and accepts the responsibility of dependence. To merit this mutuality of interests the newspaper owes and must give adherence to high standards and these recognized ideals of motive, heart, and conduct.

TRUTH AND HONESTY

The foundation stone of the profession of journalism is truth. Unwavering adherence to "whatsoever things are

[1] Written by a committee composed of J. H. McKeever, H. A. Sturges, Paul W. Kieser, and J. A. Wright, and adopted by the South Dakota Press Association in 1922.

true, whatsoever things are honest," must be the constant aim of men and women who publish newspapers.

News should be uncolored report of all vital facts accurately stated, insofar as it is possible to arrive at them.

Editorials should be sincere discussion based upon true statements in the premises from which honest argument may be developed by orderly deduction.

Advertising should be decent and honest in its selling intent and free from misleading or untrue statement.

FAIRNESS AND ACCURACY

The profession of journalism must be fair in all its dealings with the public. Society exists and our laws are made under a government deriving its powers from the people and depending upon their approval for its stability and continued existence.

To the end that this continue to be justly so, it is of first importance that the whole people be kept fully and fairly informed.

The printed word is the most widespread and useful medium of contact with the human mind, and the newspaper the most powerful agency for broad-casting information. Upon those who practice this profession rests the sacred duty of keeping these mighty means of communication among mankind pure at the source, undefiled of intent, and free of bias.

The profession of journalism is the greatest force in influencing human judgment. It is of first importance therefore, that judgments be formed after a fair presentation of all facts, accurately stated. This accuracy is not only to be an absence of misstatement, but the orderly presence of all the pertinent truths.

In accuracy partisanship or the taint of propaganda has no part and cannot be present in fair journalism.

SINCERITY AND DECENCY

Sincerity of purpose as well as of writings characterizes the ethical journalist. Honest convictions inspire his written words. Back of them is the sincerity of desire that actuates all high intent.

With full realization of this, the members of the South Dakota Press Association accept their responsibility in truthfully reporting, in directing the thoughts, and shaping the conduct of society. In all sincerity and to the utmost extent that is right and reasonable in our respective communities, we pledge our efforts to this end.

Guaranteed the freedom of its press, the profession of journalism recognizes liberty is not license. It therefore reserves to itself the right of decision in what shall be printed and what shall be omitted.

This is done to safeguard our publications from unre-finement, to protect within reason the rights and reputations of individuals, and to free our papers from sordidness, except as we sincerely believe publication to be for the good of society.

We deem suppression to be a righteous function of ethical journalism to enforce omission of undue matter based upon an honorable intent to serve public good, and not selfish purpose.

Advertising, indecent in word or motive, the aim of which is to defraud, or which serves no useful purpose, has no part in the publications of the sincere member of the profession.

HONOR

The honor of the profession is above the publication of an untruth upon an unworthy motive or upon a biased discussion based upon the false premise of a half truth entered upon for personal gain or party advancement.

The honor of the profession should be dear to all in a realization that individual character and conduct reflect good or ill upon the profession. If then, private honor never be smirched by private act or omission, the honor of the profession remains unsullied.

RECOMPENSE AND RESPECT

As the servant is worthy of his hire, journalism is entitled to fair recompense in proportion as it serves. This must be evidenced by a demand which should be sufficient to establish all useful publications upon a sound business basis.

This is a prime essential because it is a fact that the publication, successful through honest endeavor and free of entanglements of financial obligation and political debt, has broader scope toward service, freer acceptance of its opinions and a larger opportunity for usefulness. Success in service is the end sought. And it is only to be obtained rightfully through integrity, industry, and a clear vision of the function of the true journalist.

As the profession of journalism demands of its members that they be honest, fair, and just to all, they in return shall demand fair treatment, justice, and respect from those with whom they deal.

MISSOURI DECLARATION OF PRINCIPLES AND CODE OF PRACTICE [1]

PREAMBLE

In America, where the stability of the government rests upon the approval of the people, it is essential that newspapers, the medium through which the people draw their information, be developed to a high point of efficiency, stability, impartiality, and integrity. The future of the republic depends on the maintenance of a high standard among journalists. Such a standard can not be maintained unless the motives and conduct of the members of our profession are such as merit approval and confidence.

The profession of journalism is entitled to stand side by side with the other learned professions and is, far more than any other, interwoven with the lines of public service. The journalist can not consider his profession rightly unless he recognizes his obligation to the public. A newspaper does not belong solely to its owner and is not fulfilling its highest functions if devoted selfishly. Therefore the Missouri Press Association presents the following principles as a general guide, not as a set form of rules, for the practice of journalism.

EDITORIAL

We declare as a fundamental principle that Truth is the basis of all correct journalism. To suppress the truth,

[1] Written by William Southern, Jr., and adopted by the Missouri Press Association in 1921.

when it properly belongs to the public, is a betrayal of public faith.

Editorial comment should always be fair and just and not controlled by business or political expediency. Nothing should be printed editorially which the writer will not readily acknowledge as his own in public.

Control of news or comment for business considerations is not worthy of a newspaper. The news should be covered, written, and interpreted wholly and at all times in the interest of the public. Advertisers have no claim on newspaper favor except in their capacity as readers and as members of the community.

No person who controls the policy of a newspaper should at the same time hold office or have affiliations, the duties of which conflict with the public service that his newspaper should render.

ADVERTISING

It is not good ethics nor good business to accept advertisements that are dishonest, deceptive, or misleading. Concerns or individuals who want to use your columns to sell questionable stocks or anything else which promises great returns for small investment should always be investigated. Our readers should be protected from advertising sharks. Rates should be fixed at a figure which will yield a profit and never cut. The reader deserves a square deal and the advertiser the same kind of treatment.

Advertising disguised as news or editorial should not be accepted. Political advertising especially should show at a glance that it is advertising. It is just as bad to be bribed by the promise of political patronage as to be bribed by political cash.

To tear down a competitor in order to build up one's

self is not good business, nor is it ethical. Newspaper controversies should never enter newspaper columns. Good business demands the same treatment to a competitor that one would like for the competitor to give to one's self. Create new business rather than try to take away that of another.

Advertising should never be demanded from a customer simply because he has given it to another paper. Merit, product, and service should be the standard.

SUBSCRIPTION

The claiming of more subscribers than are actually on the paid list in order to secure larger advertising prices is obtaining money under false pretenses. The advertiser is entitled to know just what he is getting for his money, just what the newspaper is selling to him. Subscription lists made up at nominal prices or secured by means of premiums or contests are to be strictly avoided.

OUR CODE

In every line of journalistic endeavor we recognize and proclaim our obligation to the public, our duty to regard always the truth, to deal justly and walk humbly before the gospel of unselfish service.

KANSAS CODE OF ETHICS [1]

FOR THE PUBLISHER

In Advertising

Definition.—Advertising is news, or views, of a business or professional enterprise which leads directly to its profits or increased business.

News of the industrial or commercial development of an institution which in no way has a specific bearing upon the merits of its products is not advertising.

Besides news which leads to a profit, advertising also includes communications and reports, cards of thanks, etc., over the space of which the editor has no control. Charges for the latter become more in the nature of a penalty to restrict their publication.

Responsibility.—The authorship of an advertisement should be so plainly stated in the contract or at the end that it could not avoid catching the attention of the reader before he has left the matter.

Unsigned advertisements in the news columns should either be preceded or followed by the word "advertisement" or its abbreviation.

Freedom of space.—We hold the right of the publisher to become a broker in land, loan, rental, and mercantile transactions through his want and advertising columns, and

[1] Written by Willis E. Miller and adopted by the Kansas Editorial Association in 1910—apparently the earliest code of ethics adopted by any association of journalists.

condemn any movement of those following such lines to restrict this right of the publisher to the free sale of his space for the purpose of bringing buyer and seller together.

This shall not be construed to warrant the publisher as such in handling the details, terms, etc., of the trade, but merely in safeguarding his freedom in selling his space to bring the buyer and seller together, leaving the bargaining to the principals.

Our advertising is to bring together the buyer and the seller, and we are not concerned whether it is paid for and ordered by the producer, the consumer, or a middleman.

Acceding to any other desires on the part of traders is knocking the foundations out from under the advertising business—the freedom of space. We hold that the freedom of space (where the payment is not a question) should only be restricted by the moral decency of the advertising matter.

We hold that the freedom of space denies us the right to sign any contract with a firm which contains any restrictions against the wording of the copy which we may receive from any other firm, even to the mentioning of the goods of the first firm by name.

Compensation.—We condemn the signing of contracts carrying with them the publication of any amount of free reading matter.

We condemn the acceptance of any exchange articles, trade checks, or courtesies in payment for advertising, holding that all advertising should be paid for in cash.

We condemn the giving of secret rebates upon the established advertising rate as published.

Rates.—All advertising rates should be on a unit per thousand basis and all advertisers are entitled to a full knowledge of the circulation, not only of the quantity but also of the distribution. Statements of circulation should show the number of bona fide subscribers, the number of exchanges, the number of complimentaries, and the number sold to newsdealers, and if possible the locality of distribution, in a general way.

Position.—Position contracts should be charged a fixed percentage above the established rate of the paper, and no contracts should be signed wherein a failure to give the position required results in a greater reduction from the established rate than the position premium is greater than the established rate.

Comparisons.—We consider it beneath the dignity of a publisher to place in his columns statements which make invidious comparisons between the amount of advertising carried or the circulation of his paper and that of his competitor.

Press Agents and Unpaid Advertising.—The specific trade name of an article of commerce, or the name of a merchant, manufacturer, or professional man *with reference* to his wares, products, or labors should not be mentioned in a pure news story.

We condemn as against *moral decency* the publication of any advertisement which will obviously lead to any form of retrogression, such as private medical personals, indecent massage parlor advertisements, private matrimonial advertisements, physician's or hospital's advertisement for the care of private diseases, which carry in them any descriptive or suggestive matter of the same.

IN CIRCULATION

Definition.—Circulation is the entire list of first-hand readers of a publication and comprises the paid readers, complimentary readers, exchange readers, and advertising readers.

Compensation.—Subscriptions should be solicited and received only on a basis of cash consideration, the paper and its payment being the only elements to the transaction.

Newsdealers.—The purchase of a quantity of papers should be made outright, allowing for no return of unsold copies.

Gambling.—We condemn the practice of securing subscriptions through the sale or gift of chances.

Complimentaries.—Complimentary copies should not be sent to doctors, lawyers, ministers, postal clerks, police or court officials for news or mailing privileges.

In Estimating

Definition.—Estimating is the science of computing costs. Its conclusion is the price.

Basis.—We do not favor the establishment of a minimum rate card for advertising which would be uniform among publishers, but we do favor a more thorough understanding of the subject of costs, and commend to our members the labors of the American Printers' Cost Commission of the First International Cost Congress recently held in Chicago. Let us learn our costs and then each establish a rate card based upon our investment and the cost of production, having no consideration for the comparative ability of the advertisers to pay, or the semi-news nature of the advertisement.

Quantity Discount.—We consider it unwise to allow discounts greater than 10 per cent from the rate of first insertion for succeeding insertions.

NEWS

Definition.—News is the impartial report of the activities of mind, men, and matter which do not affend the moral sensibilities of the more enlightened people.

Lies.—We condemn as against truth:

(1) The publication of fake illustrations of men and events of news interest, however marked their similarity, without an accompanying statement that they are not real pictures of the event or person, but only suggestive imitations.

(2) The publication of fake interviews made up of the assumed views of an individual, without his consent.

(3) The publication of interviews in quotations unless the exact, approved language of the interviewed be used. When an interview is not an exact quotation it should be obvious in the reading that *only* the thought and impression of the interviewer is being reported.

(4) The issuance of fake news dispatches, whether the same have for their purpose the influencing of stock quotations, elections, or the sale of securities or merchandise. Some of the greatest advertising in the world has been stolen through news columns in the form of dispatches from unscrupulous press agents. Millions have been made on the rise and fall of stock quotations caused by newspaper lics, sent out by designing reporters.

Injustice.—We condemn as against justice:

(1) The practice of reporters making detectives and spies of themselves in their endeavors to investigate thc guilt or innocence of those under suspicion.

Reporters should not enter the domain of law in the apprehension of criminals. They should not become a detective or sweating agency for the purpose of furnishing excitement to the readers.

No suspect should have his hope of a just liberty foiled through the great prejudice which the public has formed against him because of the press verdict slyly couched in the news report, even before his arrest.

We should not even by insinuation interpret as facts our conclusions, unless by signature we become personally responsible for them. Exposition, explanation, and interpretation should be left to the field of the expert or specialist with a full consciousness of his personal responsibility.

(2) The publication of the rumors and common gossips or the assumptions of a reporter relative to a suspect pending his arrest or the final culmination of his trial. A staff of reporters is not a detective agency, and the right of a suspect to a fair and impartial trial is often confounded by a reporter's practice of printing every ill-founded rumor of which he gets wind.

Indecencies.—Classification: For the sake of clearness and order, crimes with which we will be concerned may be divided into those which offend against the *public trust* (such as bribery, defalcation, or embezzlement by a public official); those which offend against *private institutions* or *employers* (which are also often defalcations and betrayals of confidence), and crimes which offend against *private morality,* most often centering around the family relation.

(1) In dealing with the suspicions against *public officials* or trustees we urge that *only facts* put in their *true relation* and records be used in the news reports.

No presumption or conclusion of the reporter should be allowed to enter, even though it has all the elements of a correct conclusion.

Conclusions and presumptions should be placed in interviews with the identity of their author easily apparent.

If an editor desires to draw a conclusion on the case, let him sign it. Do not hide behind the impersonality of the paper with your personal opinions.

(2) In dealing with the suspicions against agents of private institutions, facts alone, put in their true relation, should again be used.

But in this class of stories suspicions and conclusions should be confined to those of the parties directly interested, and no statement of one party to the affair reflecting upon another should be published without at the same time publishing a statement of the accused relative thereto.

The comment of those not directly involved should not be published previous to the arrest or pending the trial.

(3) In dealing with the offenses against private morality, we should refuse to print any record of the matter, however true, until the warrant has been filed or the arrest made, and even then our report should contain only an epitome of the charges by the plaintiff and the answers by the defendant, preferably secured from their respective attorneys.

No society gossips or scandals, however true, should ever be published concerning such cases.

However prominent the principals, offenses against private morality should never receive *first-page position* and their details should be eliminated as much as possible.

Certain crimes against private morality which are revolting to our finer sensibilities should be ignored entirely; however, in the event of their having become public with harmful exaggerations, we may make an elementary statement, couched in the least suggestive language.

In no case should the reckless daring of the suspect be lionized.

(4) Except when the suspect has escaped, his picture should never be printed.

FOR THE EDITOR

VIEWS

Definition.—Views are the impressions, beliefs, or opinions which are published in a paper, whether from the editorial staffs of the same, outside contributors, or secured interviews.

A Distinction.—We hold that whenever a publication confines the bulk of its views to any particular line of thought, class of views, or side of a moot question, it becomes to that extent a class publication, and insomuch ceases to be a newspaper.

An Explanation.—You will note by our definition of news that it is the impartial portrayal of the decent activities of mind, men, and matter. This definition applied to class publications would be changed by replacing the word *impartial* with the word *partial*.

In this section we will deal with *impartiality* in the presentation of the decent activities of the mind of the community—with the views or editorial policy of a paper.

Responsibility.—Whereas a view or conclusion is the product of some mind or minds, and whereas the value and significance of a view is dependent upon the known merit of its author or authors, the reader is entitled and has the right to know the personal identity of the author, whether by the signature in a communication, the statement of the reporter in an interview, or the caption in a special article,

and *the paper as such* should in no wise become an advocate.

Influence (Editorial).—We should avoid permitting large
institutions or persons to own stock in or make loans to our
publishing business if we have reasonable grounds to believe that their interest would be seriously affected by any
other than a true presentation of all news and free willingness to present every possible point of view under signature
or interview.

Influence (Reportorial).—No reporter should be retained
who accepts any courtesies, unusual favors, opportunities
for self-gain, or side employment from any factors whose
interests would be affected by the manner in which his reports are made.

Deception.—We should not allow the *presumed* knowledge on the part of the interviewed that we are newspaper
men to permit us to quote them without their explicit permission, but where such knowledge is certain we insist upon
our right to print the views unless directly forbidden.

Faith With Interviewed.—An interview or statement
should not be displayed previous to its publication without
the permission of the author.

Bounds of Publicity.—A man's name and portrait are his
private property and the point where they cease to be
private and become public should be defined for our association.

EXTRACTS FROM RULES AND SUGGESTIONS PREPARED BY NEWSPAPERS FOR THE GUIDANCE OF THEIR STAFFS [1]

THE BROOKLYN EAGLE

EAGLE POLICY

1. *The Brooklyn Eagle* is primarily a home newspaper. It prints all the news, but aims to emphasize what is helpful rather than harmful. It believes in enterprise, but not in sensationalism. As a 3-cent newspaper it must uphold the highest standards of newspaper making. In particular it must always be truthful, accurate and fair.

2. "Brooklyn First" is a cardinal principle of *Eagle* policy. This newspaper is a Brooklyn institution. It is also a public service institution. Whatever helps Brooklyn helps *The Eagle*. The more you know about Brooklyn and about *The Eagle* the better you will serve both.

3. *The Eagle* ranks as one of the world's greatest newspapers. The world is its province and its interest extends to the activities of human-kind everywhere. It is through being liberal and cosmopolitan that you can best contribute your share to preserving *The Eagle's* reputation as a broadly representative newspaper.

GENERAL RULES

The cardinal principle of good newspaper work is accuracy. *The Eagle* demands it and will insist on getting it.

[1] A number of newspapers have no such published rules, but depend on tradition and oral instruction.

Verify your facts. Don't depend on some one's say-so, but go to the reference books.

Get names right. Nothing does a newspaper more harm than misspelled names. A list of names frequently used in *The Eagle* is included in this book. Supplement this with a list of your own. Carelessness in this connection always bars promotion and has led to dismissal.

Be fair. *The Eagle* wants to make friends, not enemies. Don't suppress any part of the truth for fear of spoiling a good story. Get both sides. Don't let any one use *The Eagle* to vent a grudge. Give the man or institution under attack a chance to make out a case.

When a person is charged with crime or has done something immoral or discreditable do not intrude the names of prominent relatives who are in no way involved. In writing obituaries do not emphasize unfortunate incidents in the lives of well-reputed persons.

Beware of the seekers after free publicity. Remember that space in *The Eagle* is worth twenty-five cents a line. What you give away *The Eagle* cannot sell. Don't help press agents cheat the advertising department.

Always hesitate to write anything that will offend the members of a race or sect. You may offend 20,000 *Eagle* readers with a single word. Do not mention the nationality or religious belief of a person under arrest unless that is an essential and inevitable feature of the story. Don't emphasize locality in fire or burglary stories or in news reports which give a special section an unsavory reputation.

Read *The Eagle* from the first page to the last. Only in that way can you become familiar with its style, its policy, and its special hobbies. If you discover errors, report them; if you have suggestions, make them. Read the other local papers and note how they handled your story. If you notice any important difference of fact, length or emphasis, call it to the City Editor's attention. To be known as a "live wire" is to be in line for promotion.

Beware of your own prejudices. Your personal likes or dislikes have no place in a news story. If you feel strongly on some subject try your hand at an editorial or write a letter for the Forum Page. But keep your news reports free from editorial comment.

Never promise to suppress a news story. News which you secure as an *Eagle* employee is *The Eagle's* property, and your superiors are the final judges of what shall or shall not be used. Requests for suppression or omission must always be carefully reported and reasons given, but your answer to the request must be nothing more than the promise that you will transmit it.

Always accept news items or suggestions from outsiders gratefully. Some may be worthless, but an attitude of encouragement ultimately wins help that will prove invaluable to you and to *The Eagle*.

THE CHRISTIAN SCIENCE MONITOR

1. *Good English.*—A feature of *The Monitor* is the wide field covered in its news service and the various departments; therefore space in its columns is valuable—each word should be to the point and tell its own story.

2. Terse, crisp writing is not necessarily devoid of the picturesque, and is far more forceful. In three words, "boil it down."

3. Aim at simplicity; express your thoughts so clearly "he that runs may read." Faulty construction; long, involved sentences, in which the original subject and predicate are hopelessly entangled in a labyrinth of modifying phrases and clauses, and the pronouns have become of doubtful lineage—all these are faults to be avoided. Use words of one syllable rather than those of many—the latter may serve to show off your learning, but the average reader hasn't a dictionary at his elbow or the time to use it.

4. You are writing for an English-reading public, of whom only a minority are college-bred men and women—don't lose sight of the majority. It often happens that the exact shade of meaning—it may be the pith of your "story"—can be conveyed only in the original tongue—use it then, by all means; but as a rule only such foreign words and expressions as by long and familiar usage have become a part of the English language have any place in the columns of a daily paper.

5. *Nauseating words.*—Never use expressions that suggest nauseating ideas; as "burned to a crisp," "gutted."

6. Avoid such tautological expressions as "marriage nuptials," "funeral obsequies," "suffocated to death," etc.

7. *Slang.*—Slang is undoubtedly a large element in colloquial language, yet it must be excluded from the columns of *The Christian Science Monitor.* Even in interviews it must not be used unless sanctioned by the EDITOR-IN-CHIEF. When the paper speaks for itself the use of slang is prohibited. This caution is given the second time that all may mark its imperative nature.

8. *News, not Opinions.*—The news columns are for news; not for opinions except as these are reported as news. Attempts on the part of the reporters or correspondents to usurp the editor's functions and pass judgment upon the merits of propositions should be suppressed, no matter how big a hole the omission makes in the story.

9. Beware of imputations of wrong-doing in connection with mysterious disappearances. Comment is not justifiable unless public interests are involved, and then good authority should be had for any statements made.

10. Reports of failures or anything affecting commercial credit should never be used upon hearsay.

11. *Accuracy.*—Editors and reporters in preparing their "copy" must write PROPER NAMES so plainly that they NEED NOT BE mistaken, and also when possible should use printed matter in the casts of plays and programs. One of the primal points in satisfactory performance of duty for *The Christian Science Monitor* is accuracy. This is made possible in the various departments by competent work in the editorial and reportorial branches. Write out in full both the first and last names of persons; initial for middle name.

12. Verify all quotations, especially from the Bible, whenever time will permit.

13. *Heads.*—Indicate style of head by number. Make careful count, so that the head as written may fit the style. Head-lines must be an index to the story, not a characterization of it; descriptive, not opinionated; concrete, not abstract; and alliteration, claptrap, and sensationalism are PROHIBITED. General headings such as "Held for Court," "Sent to Jail," "Sued for Damages," will not be tolerated. Avoid such headings as "Killed Her Own Children"; "Frantic Mother's Horrible Deed"; "Lake Steamer Lost in Storm"; "Wild Waves Gather a Harvest of Death."

15. *Above All.*—Remember that you are preparing copy for a Christian Science publication whose standard is Truth and whose policy is absolutely devoid of sensationalism.

THE SPRINGFIELD REPUBLICAN

Interviewing

Never put within quotation marks in your copy what people say to you in an interview without,

First—An understanding with them that they are to be quoted.

Second—Letting them know just what words you attribute to them.

This is the only safe rule to follow when the subject is at all controversial or involves private or personal interests.

When people are quoted, the paper is placed in the position of assuring its readers that the quoted passages were literally spoken; consequently, inaccuracy in quotation is unpardonable.

Direct quotation in an interview, unless permission is given to use that form, can be avoided ordinarily by using indirect discourse. For instance, you may write: Mr. Smith, in discussing the subject, said in effect that—etc.

Reports of public addresses should never be put within quotation marks unless the exact language of the speaker is reproduced.

Before interviewing a person, decide on a series of questions on the subject about which you wish to inquire. If the person interviewed talks willingly, follow him through. If he does not, stick to your original questions. If the assignment presents difficulties, before you attempt it consult the city editor about the best method to pursue. Try to familiarize yourself as much as possible with the subject about which you are to talk with him.

OBITUARIES

Be very careful about writing obituaries. Make every possible effort to get the facts and write them accurately. Omit reference to aspects of the dead person's life, unless the circumstances are exceptional, which would pain or aggrieve the surviving relatives and friends. Good will may be cultivated for the paper by writing appreciatively of the dead person's good qualities and achievements.

MISCELLANEOUS INSTRUCTIONS

Read over your article so as to be sure the reader will get the picture you have in mind.

Do not depend on the editor to correct your mistakes; correct them yourself.

Never try to write a humorous article on the suffering or death of an animal; nor, in the case of human beings, where the incident involves disgrace, humiliation, or sorrow to them, their relatives, or friends.

Carefully estimate every piece of news you get. There is ample space for important news. Unimportant news should be disposed of as briefly as possible.

Wrong things will from time to time be done and wrong conditions will develop in this as in every other community. It is the function of an honest newspaper to print the news without fear or favor. Publicity brings correction. But no report should be so written that it can be interpreted as revealing a petty malice on the part of the reporter or the paper in attributing wrongful acts to any person. *The Republican* has been published in Springfield for nearly

100 years; it believes, with pride, that the standards of the community are high and that it has contributed to their maintenance by a fearless news policy. *The Republican,* however, is not out to "get" anybody in order to gratify animosities. The paper wants friends, not enemies.

THE SPRINGFIELD UNION

1. *The Union* aims to be a newspaper worth while, a newspaper that will make you feel that you have rendered the public some measure of service.

2. Strive to be accurate and fair in your statements, that *The Union* may print the truth without bias.

3. Write nothing as a journalist that you would not write as a gentleman.

4. Seek to get news of real public interest. Give to it the space it is actually worth and a heading that will indicate its relative importance.

5. Remember, this is a busy world and few persons have the time or inclination to read verbose accounts of happenings, however important.

6. Tell what you have to tell in clear, concise English, attaching to words their true meanings.

7. Do not dwell on human frailties, or try to make sensations out of things that are not sensational. If you cry wolf when there is no wolf, the public will not believe you when the wolf comes. Public confidence is the best asset a newspaper can have, and it is your best asset also.

8. Avoid all that is yellow in journalism, but emulate the enterprise that characterizes the yellow journalist.

9. Regard as especially valuable news concerning the world's progress—news of discoveries in the arts and sciences, news of inventions likely to work important changes, news of enterprises in which labor is interested, news of financial institutions and large corporations, news

of railroads and all other public utilities, news of real estate transactions, news relating to public improvements, news of outdoor and indoor sports and pastimes, news concerning well-known persons, news pertaining to educational and religious topics, news of a political nature—in short, all news that naturally appeals to wholesome-minded people desirous of being informed of what is going on around and about them.

10. Put yourself in the reader's place and ask "Will this interest the average reader, and if so, how many of him?" Your judgment of your readers will be reflected in the way your story is written, in the amount of space you give to it and in the heading that you put on it.

11. To be on the safe side try to get as many different items as possible into *The Union,* remembering that *The Union* is read by many people of varying tastes.

ACCURACY AND FAIRNESS

Accuracy! *The Union* demands it and will insist on getting it. Every correspondent, every reporter, every copy-reader, every editor, must learn to be accurate. And it is not enough merely to be accurate. It is quite as essential to be fair. Partial truths are worse than lies. Tell the truth, the whole truth, and nothing but the truth.

Don't accept anybody's say-so for the facts. See everybody concerned; get all sides. Something may seem to be so, probably is so, but you will not know whether it really is so until you have found out for yourself. Don't supply details from your imagination.

Nothing in all the world is so interesting as facts. If you write facts and write them fairly you can laugh at libel suits.

The Union makes due allowances for mistakes; it realizes

that they occasionally will occur, but it expects every member of its staff to profit by his mistakes and not repeat them.
Chronic carelessness invariably will result in dismissal. If
you can't get things right *The Union* doesn't want you.

Inaccuracy does serious injury to innocent persons, it
hurts your chances of promotion and it destroys the public's
confidence in the newspaper. The Union wants its readers
to feel that they can believe everything it prints.

Be accurate.

Be fair.

Get facts.

SOME OF THE UNION'S POLICIES

1. *The Union* aims to be a constructive, not a destructive
newspaper. Get the news, but be charitable.

2. In politics *The Union* is Republican, but not narrowly
so. It believes in the broad underlying principles of the
Republican party, but does not feel in any way bound to
support every measure advocated by that party nor every
candidate running on the Republican ticket. It puts the
common good ahead of party or other considerations. It
aims to deal fairly with all political parties, to give the
news regardless of its own opinions, and to keep its columns
always open. It is a newspaper absolutely free from en-
tangling alliances of any sort.

3. *The Union* does not print the names of children who
get into trouble with the police nor give publicity to cases
that come before the juvenile court, unless the circumstances are such as to afford abundant justification for so
doing.

4. *The Union* does not publish the names of persons arrested for drunkenness, nor of "drunks" who are fined
nominal amounts by the court, unless the arrest and appear-

ance in court were attended by unusual circumstances. Give them a chance to reform.

5. *The Union* does not mention the nationality of a person that commits a crime or other discreditable act, except as that may be an essential detail of the affair. The name itself usually conveys sufficient information and other persons of the same race quite properly resent the added emphasis that mention of the nationality gives.

6. It is *The Union's* policy to report cases of suicide in the briefest manner possible, unless the circumstances are very extraordinary or the person is of particular prominence. If death was accomplished by poison, do not name the kind of poison used. If with a revolver, do not tell where the bullet struck. If by hanging, do not describe the method. Do not make the account suggest to those who may be contemplating self-destruction how they may go about it.

7. In automobile accidents do not give the name of the car, nor in shooting cases the make of weapon used.

8. Do not advertise anything in the news columns. Articles offered for free publication are always to be regarded with suspicion. Generally they are clever attempts to get advertising for nothing. Don't help publicity agents to cheat the advertising department.

THE DETROIT NEWS

The paper should be:

Vigorous, but not Vicious.

Interesting, but not Sensational.

Fearless, but Fair.

Accurate as far as human effort can obtain accuracy.

Striving ever to gain and impart information.

As bright as possible, but never sacrificing solid information for brilliancy.

Looking for the Uplifting rather than the Depraved things of Life.

We should work to have the word *reliable* stamped all over every page of the paper.

The place to commence this is with the staff members: First getting men and women of character to do the writing and editing, and then training them in our way of thinking and handling news and other reading matter.

Nothing here is intended as a reflection on the present staff or the paper we have been getting out; we have a good staff and a good paper; the aim is to improve both as much as possible.

If you make an error, you have two duties to perform: One to the person misrepresented and one to your reading public. Never leave the reader of *The News* misinformed on any subject. If you wrongfully infer that a man has done something that he did not do, or has said something that he did not say, you do him an injustice—that's one. But you also do thousands of readers an injustice, leaving them misinformed as to the character of the man dealt with. Corrections should never be given grudgingly. Always make them cheerfully, fully, and in larger type than the error, if any difference.

If a reporter gets drunk, the people do not say, "There goes So-and-So," calling him by name; they say, "There goes a *News* reporter." That reflects on the entire staff; that robs the paper of a certain amount of its standing, of a certain amount of its reputation for reliability. No one has confidence in the work of a drunken man. Any one on the editorial staff who gets drunk once or who wilfully prints a misstatement of any kind should not be retained on the staff a minute.

The American people want to *know*, to learn, to get information. To quote a writer: "Your opinion is worth no more than your information." Give them your information and let them draw their own conclusions. Comment should be more along the line of enlightenment by well-marshalled facts, and by telling the readers what relation an act of today has to an act of yesterday. Let them come to their own conclusions as far as possible.

No issue is worth advocating that is not strong enough to withstand all the facts that the opposition to it can throw against it. Our readers should be well informed on both sides of *every* issue.

Kindly, helpful suggestions will often direct officials in the right, where nagging will make them stay stubbornly on the wrong side. That does not mean that there should be any lack of diligence in watching for, and opposition to, intentional crooks.

A staff can only be good and strong by having every part of it strong. The moment it becomes evident that a man, either by force of circumstance or because of his own character, does not fit into our organization, you do him a kindness and do justice to the paper by letting him know, so he can go to a calling in which he can succeed, and he will not be in the way of filling the place with a competent man.

Make the paper good all the way through, so there will not be disappointment on the part of a reporter if his story is not found on the first page, but so he will feel it must have merit to get into the paper at all. Avoid making it a "front-page paper."

Stories should be brief, but not meager. Tell the story, all of it, in as few words as possible.

Nature makes facts more interesting than any reporter can imagine them. There is an interesting feature in every story, if you will but dig it out. If you don't get it, it is because you don't dig deep enough.

The most valuable asset of any paper is its reputation for telling the truth; the only way to have that reputation is to tell the truth. Untruth, due to carelessness, or excessive imagination, injures the paper as much as though intentional.

Everyone with a complaint should be given a respectful and kindly hearing; especial consideration should be given the poor and lowly, who may be less able to present their claims than those more favored in life. A man of prominence and education knows how to get into the office and present his complaint. A washerwoman may come to the door, timidly, haltingly, scarcely knowing what to do, and all the while her complaint may be as just as that of the other complainant, perhaps more so. She should be received kindly and helped to present what she has to say.

Simple, plain language is strongest and best. A man of meager education can understand it, while the man of higher education, usually reading a paper in the evening after a day's work, will read it with relish. There is never any need of using big words to show off one's learning. The object of a story or an editorial is to inform or convince; but it is hard to do either if the reader has to study over a big word or an involved sentence. Stick to plain English all the time. A few readers may understand and appreciate a Latin or French quotation, or one from some other foreign language, but the big mass of our readers are the plain people and such a quotation would be lost on the majority.

Be fair. Don't let the libel laws be your measure as to the printing of a story, but let fairness be your measure. If you are fair, you need not worry any about libel laws.

Always give the other fellow a hearing. He may be in the wrong, but even that may be a matter of degree. It wouldn't be fair to picture him as all black when there may be mitigating circumstances.

It is not necessary to tell the people that we are honest, or bright, or alert, or that a story appeared exclusively in our paper. If true, the public will find it out. An honest man does not have to advertise his honesty eternally.

Time heals all things but a woman's damaged reputation. Be careful and cautious and fair and decent in dealing with any man's reputation, but be doubly so—and then some—when a woman's name is at stake. Do not by direct statement, jest, or careless reference, raise a question mark after any woman's name if it can be avoided—and it usually can be. Even if a woman slips, be generous; it may be a crisis in her life. Printing the story may drive her to despair; kindly treatment may leave her with hope. No story is worth ruining a woman's life—or man's either.

Keep the paper clean in language and thought. Profane or suggestive words are not necessary. When in doubt, think of a 13-year-old girl reading what you are writing.

Do not look on newspaper work as a "game," of pitilessly printing that on which you are only half-informed, for the mere sake of beating some other paper, but take it rather as a serious, constructive work in which you are to use all the energy and diligence needed to get all the worth-while information for your readers at the earliest possible moment at which you can do so and have it reliable.

Nothing should ever be taken from another publication without giving full credit. Merely crediting a piece of writing to "Exchange" is not fair.

Elections coming on Tuesday, no candidate or party should be permitted to print new charges or statements later than the Friday before election. No paper should print anything about anybody without allowing ample time for an answer.

The hardest lesson the journalist must learn is the development of the impersonal viewpoint. He must learn to write what he sees and hears, clearly and accurately, with never a tinge of bias. His own views, his personal feelings, and his friendships should have nothing to do with what he writes in a story.

The ideal reporter would be a man who could give the public facts about his bitterest enemy even though such facts would make the man he personally hated a hero before the public.

THE HEARST NEWSPAPERS [1]

ADVERTISING

The principles and policies governing the advertising department of our newspapers should be just as firmly established and just as well known to every one in the business office as the news and editorial departments.

News and editorial character are built only on reliability of statement. We cannot hope to build advertising on any other basis. No man who misrepresents facts must be allowed on our newspapers. Honesty is a form of common sense.

Employ men of brains, breeding and acquaintance. Character counts in advertising as in all other things.

Our newspapers must sell advertising only by their printed rate card. If your rate card is wrong, change it. If it is right, live up to every letter of it. There should be no double standard of morality involving buyer and seller of advertising. Cut rates, special concessions and secret rebates are boomerangs, which return to cripple progress when they are least expected. Men who make "gentlemen's agreements" are not wanted.

Do not accept any advertising which is detrimental to the public welfare. Questionable financial, objectionable medical, clairvoyants, spiritualists, fortune tellers and fake

[1] The selections are from the personal instructions given by William Randolph Hearst to his newspapers.

229

advertising of any and every description have no place in
the Hearst newspapers. Our readers trust us. We would
not deceive them in our news or editorial columns. We
must not allow others to deceive them in our advertising
columns.

NEWS

Make the paper *accurate and trustworthy.*

Compare statements in our paper with those in other
papers and find out which are accurate.

Get rid of reporters and copy-readers who are per-
sistently inaccurate. Reward those who are trustworthy as you reward those who are valuable in other
respects.

Don't allow exaggeration. It is a cheap and ineffective
substitute for real interest. Show appreciation for reporters *who can make the truth interesting.* Eliminate
those who can not.

Be fair and impartial in the news columns at least.
Don't make a paper for Democrats, or Republicans, or Independence Leaguers. Make a paper for all the people,
and give unbiased news of all creeds and parties. Try to
do this in such a conspicuous manner that it will *be noticed*
and *commented* upon.

Condense the news when necessary to get it in. Much
of the news is *better* when *intelligently condensed.*

Make your departments complete and reliable, so that
the reader will know, first, that he can find a thing in the
paper, and, second, that he can find it right.

Make the paper *thorough;* print all the news. Not only
get all the news into the office, but see that it gets into the
paper.

Select the *best stories* in the paper and *feature* them—

i. e., emphasize them in a way to make them stand out and give life and character to the paper.

If your feature is big enough, it must get *display, regardless of everything;* but mere display does not make a feature.

It is *not necessary to cover a page with a story* in order to make it a feature. A page feature generally looks heavy and is heavy. A story should be made to stand out by *appreciation* of the interesting points and *emphasis* of those points in typography and phraseology. A feature *can* be made interesting in a column, and it may be made stupid in a page.

Make a paper *for the best kind of people.* The masses of the reading public are better and more intelligent than newspapermen seem to think they are.

Don't print a lot of stuff that nice people are supposed to like and do not, but omit things that will offend nice people.

Avoid *coarseness* and *slang* and a *low tone.* The most sensational news can be told if it is written properly.

Don't use the words "murder," "scandal," "divorce," "crime," and other rather offensive phrases when it is possible to tell the story without them. Murder stories and other criminal stories are not printed merely because they are *criminal,* but because of the *mystery,* or the *romance,* or the *dramatic qualities* in them. Therefore, develop the *mystery,* or the *romance,* or the *dramatic qualities,* and avoid the offensive qualities.

Make the paper helpful and kindly and pleasing.

Don't scold and forever complain and attack in the news columns.

An occasionable justifiable crusade or exposure will be all the more effective if this rule is maintained.

Please sum up your paper every day at a conference and find wherein it is *distinctly better* than the other papers. If it is not distinctly better, you have *missed that day*. Lay out p!ans to make it distinctly better the next day.

THE SACRAMENTO BEE

The Bee demands from all its writers accuracy before anything else. Better lose an item than make a splurge one day and correct it next.

Equally with that, it demands absolute fairness in the treatment of news. Reports must not be colored to please a friend or wrong an enemy.

Don't editorialize in the news columns. An accurate report is its own best editorial.

Don't exaggerate. Every exaggeration hurts immeasurably the cause it pretends to help.

If a mistake is made, it must be corrected. It is as much the duty of a *Bee* writer to work to the rectification of a wrong done by an error in an item as it is first to use every precaution not to allow that error to creep in.

Be extremely careful of the name and reputation of women. Even when dealing with the unfortunate, remember that so long as she commits no crime other than her own sin against chastity, she is entitled at least to pity.

Sneers at race, or religion, or physical deformity, will not be tolerated. "Dago," "Mick," "Sheeny," even "Chink" or "Jap," these are absolutely forbidden. This rule of regard for the feelings of others must be observed in every avenue of news, under any and all conditions.

There is a time for humor and there is a time for seriousness. *The Bee* likes snap and ginger at all times. It will not tolerate flippancy on serious subjects on any occasion.

The furnisher of an item is entitled to a hearing for his

side at all times, not championship.   If the latter is ever deemed necessary, the editorial department will attend to it.

Interviews given the paper at the paper's request are to be considered immune from sneers or criticism.

In every accusation against a public official or private citizen, make every effort to have the statement of the accused given prominence in the original item.

In the case of charges which are not ex officio or from a public source, it is better to lose an item than to chance the doing of a wrong.

Consider *The Bee* always as a tribunal that desires to do justice to all; that fears far more to do injustice to the poorest beggar than to clash swords with wealthy injustice.

THE SEATTLE TIMES

The following rules of decency are published for the guidance of all concerned:

(a) Remember that young girls read *The Times.*
(b) The physiology of conception and childbirth and all matters relating thereto will not be discussed in the columns of *The Times.*
(c) All scandalous matter will be omitted, excepting where competent orders are given to the contrary.
(d) When it is necessary to refer to improper relations between the sexes, the limit permitted in *The Times* is some such statement as: "The couple were divorced," or "The couple separated," or "Various charges were made not considered fit for publication in the columns of *The Times.*"
(e) The use of the words, "rape," "adultery," "indecent exposure," "incest," "assault" (in this connection), or any word, phrase, or sentence, similar or having like meaning, is prohibited.
(f) As far as practicable, any news bearing upon events that depend upon the commission of crimes of sex will be omitted from the paper. Where a person is lynched for a crime against a woman or child, the cause of the lynching will not be given, and for it will be substituted some such statement as "The victim of the mob was accused of injuring a woman."
(g) Reference to expectancy of motherhood or physi-

cians' certificates in connection with establishment of the innocence of a woman charged with a sexual crime, or any other subject that in the remotest degree is of a similar character, will be omitted.

(h) In connection with accidents where persons are injured or killed, all unpleasant details of suffering or maiming will be omitted. In this connection the word "mangle" is forbidden, and this prohibition should carry with it by inference anything of a similar nature.

THE KANSAS CITY JOURNAL-POST

There are two sides to every story. GET BOTH.

The best story is simply told and told simply.

Be truthful.

Get the facts.

The Journal-Post will play its politics on the editorial page. Write political stories impartially.

Treat religious matters reverently.

Avoid heaping ignominy on innocent men, women, and children.

The Journal-Post's ideals are high—truthfulness, toleration, fairness, decency, and cleanliness.

ALWAYS VERIFY NAMES!

THE MARION STAR [1]

Remember there are two sides to every question. Get them both.

Be truthful.

Get the facts. Mistakes are inevitable, but strive for accuracy. I would rather have one story exactly right than a hundred half wrong.

Be decent. Be fair. Be generous.

Boost—don't knock. There's good in everybody. Bring out the good and never needlessly hurt the feelings of anybody.

In reporting a political gathering, get the facts: Tell the story as it is, not as you would like to have it.

Treat all parties alike. If there is any politics to be played, we will play them in our editorial columns.

Treat all religious matters reverently.

If it can possibly be avoided, never bring ignominy on an innocent man or child, in telling of the misdeeds or misfortunes of a relative. Don't wait to be asked, but do it without the asking.

And, above all, be clean. Never let a dirty word or suggestive story get into type.

I want this paper to be so conducted that it can go into any home without destroying the innocence of any child.

[1] Written by the late President Warren G. Harding when editing *The Star*.

THE JOURNALIST'S CREED

By Walter Williams

I believe in the profession of journalism.

I believe that the public journal is a public trust; that all connected with it are, to the full measure of their responsibility, trustees for the public; that acceptance of lesser service than the public service is betrayal of this trust.

I believe that clear thinking, and clear statement, accuracy, and fairness are fundamental to good journalism.

I believe that a journalist should write only what he holds in his heart to be true.

I believe that suppression of the news for any consideration other than the welfare of society is indefensible.

I believe that no one should write as a journalist what he would not say as a gentleman; that bribery by one's own pocketbook is as much to be avoided as bribery by the pocketbook of another; that individual responsibility may not be escaped by pleading another's instruction or another's dividends.

I believe that advertising, news, and editorial columns should alike serve the best interests of the readers; that a single standard of helpful truth and clearness should prevail for all; that the supreme test of journalism is the measure of its public service.

I believe that the journalism which succeeds best—and the best deserves success—fears God and honors man; is stoutly independent, unmoved by pride of opinion, or greed of power; constructive, tolerant, but never careless; self-controlled, patient, always respectful of its readers, always unafraid; is quickly indignant at injustice; is unswayed by the appeal of privilege, or the clamor of the mob; seeks to give every man a chance, and, as far as law and honest wages and recognition of human brotherhood can make it so, an equal chance; is profoundly patriotic, while sincerely promoting international good will, and cementing world comradeship; is a journalism of humanity, of and for today's world.

APPENDIX B

A SELECTIVE BIBLIOGRAPHY

BOOKS AND PARTS OF BOOKS

Adams, Samuel Hopkins. *The Clarion.* Boston: Houghton
Mifflin Company. 1914.
A novel dealing with the newspaper and the patent medicine
business.

Adams, Samuel Hopkins. *The Great American Fraud.* Chicago: American Medical Association. 1906.
Articles on the patent medicine business and its influence on
the press.

Adams, Samuel Hopkins. *Success.* Boston: Houghton Mifflin Company. 1921.
A novel of newspaper life, bringing out many ethical
problems.

American Bar Association. *Canons of Professional Ethics.*
Baltimore: American Bar Association. 1917.
A statement of the ethical standards of the American bar.

American Medical Association. *Principles of Medical Ethics.*
Chicago: American Medical Association. 1914.
A statement of the ethical principles held in the medical pro-
fession in the United States.

Angell, Norman. *The Press and the Organisation of Society.*
London: Labour Publishing Company. 1922.
A study of the press in relation to social organization, from
the intellectual labor point of view.

Audit Bureau of Circulations. *Scientific Space Selection.*
Chicago: Audit Bureau of Circulations. 1921.
A detailed explanation of the basis of the sale of advertising
space, with data on its evolution.

Belloc, Hilaire. *The Free Press.* London: George Allen &
Unwin, Ltd. 1918.
An analysis of the effects of commercialism on the British

press, and a discussion of the "free press" as a means for making the truth known.

Bennett, Arnold. *What the Public Wants.* New York: George H. Doran Company. 1911.

A play dealing with an English newspaper proprietor who has no ideal above that of pleasing the public.

Bleyer, Willard Grosvenor, *editor. The Profession of Journalism.* Boston: Atlantic Monthly Press. 1918.

Essays on various phases of journalism, by various writers, originally published in *The Atlantic Monthly.*

Chafee, Zechariah, Jr. *Freedom of Speech.* New York: Harcourt, Brace and Howe. 1920.

A discussion, by a distinguished professor of law, of the historic meaning of freedom of speech and of recent departures from that meaning.

Chicago Commission on Race Relations. *The Negro in Chicago,* pp. 436–574, 629–639, 650–651. Chicago: University of Chicago Press. 1922.

Data on the handling of race riot news by the press, and recommendations with reference to public opinion on the negro problem.

Cook, E. T. *The Press in Wartime.* New York: The Macmillan Company. 1920.

A detailed discussion, by a British writer, of the situation of the press in war.

Dana, Charles. *The Art of Newspaper Making.* New York: D. Appleton and Company. 1895.

Three lectures giving the views of the distinguished nineteenth-century editor on ethical and other problems of journalism.

Davis, Elmer. *History of The New York Times, 1851–1921.* New York: The New York Times. 1921.

A history of one of the greatest newspapers in the United States, by a member of its editorial staff.

Eastman, Max. *Journalism Versus Art.* New York: Alfred A. Knopf, Inc. 1916.

Criticism of the influence of journalism against significant art.

Edman, Irwin. *Human Traits and Their Social Significance*. Boston: Houghton Mifflin Company. 1920.
A discussion of human traits in the contemporary social environment.

Every-day Ethics, pp. 1–15. New Haven: Yale University press. 1910.
An address on ethical problems in journalism, delivered by Norman Hapgood at the Sheffield Scientific School.

Freud, Sigmund. *A General Introduction to Psychoanalysis*. New York: The Macmillan Company. 1922.
A work devoting much attention to the place of the emotions in the formation of beliefs.

Gibbs, Sir Philip. *Now It Can Be Told*. New York: Harper & Brothers. 1920.
A recital of facts about the Great War, showing the part played by untruthful propaganda.

Hackett, Francis. *The Invisible Censor*. New York: B. W. Huebsch, Inc. 1921.
A book of essays, some of which have special reference to journalism and public opinion.

Hale, William G. *The Law of the Press*. St. Paul: West Publishing Co. 1923.
A thorough discussion of the various laws governing the newspaper in the United States.

Hart, Bernard. *The Psychology of Insanity*. Cambridge, England: University Press. 1916.
A work on mental conflict, making clear the problems of fear, dissociation of consciousness, and the like.

Heaton, John L. *The Story of a Page*. New York: Harper & Brothers. 1913.
A history of the editorial influence of *The New York World* under Joseph Pulitzer.

Holt, Hamilton. *Commercialism and Journalism*. Boston: Houghton Mifflin Company. 1909.

An address delivered at the University of California.

Interchurch World Movement, Commission of Inquiry. *Public Opinion and the Steel Strike.* New York: Harcourt, Brace & Company. 1921.

Reports of investigators on the manipulation of public opinion, by newspapers and other means, in the steel strike of 1919.

Labour Research Department. *The Press.* London: Labour Publishing Company. 1922.

A survey of the newspaper industry as a part of the economic development of England.

Lee, James Melvin. *History of American Journalism.* Boston: Houghton Mifflin Company. 1917. Second Edition (revised), 1923.

A history containing innumerable quotations from newspapers and other valuable reference data.

Lippmann, Walter. *Liberty and the News.* New York: Harcourt, Brace and Howe. 1920.

Three essays analyzing the nature of modern liberty and its relation to the press.

Lippmann, Walter. *Public Opinion.* New York: Harcourt, Brace and Company. 1922.

The best and most modern realistic presentation of the formation of public opinion.

Locard, Edmond. *L'Enquête Criminelle et les Méthodes Scientifiques.* Paris: Ernest Flammarion. 1920.

A work showing among other things, the inability of the average witness to describe objectively.

Lowell, A. Lawrence. *Public Opinion in War and Peace.* Cambridge: Harvard University Press. 1923.

A discussion, by the president of Harvard University, of factors influencing opinion and of the reciprocal influence of opinion upon these factors.

Massart, Jean. *The Secret Press in Belgium.* New York: E. P. Dutton & Company. 1919.

A history of the maintenance of a pro-Belgian press

throughout the war despite the efforts of the German army to suppress it.

Masters, Edgar Lee. *Spoon River Anthology.* New York: The Macmillan Company. 1914.

A series of poems in which reference is made to newspapers and public opinion in a village.

Migne, Jacques Paul, *editor. Patres Latini,* Volume XIV. Paris: Garnier Frères.

St. Ambrose's |*Hexaëmeron,* which expresses the traditional attitude toward objective facts, is found in the volume cited.

Mill, John Stuart. *On Liberty.* New York: Henry Holt & Company. 1882.

A discussion, perhaps the best in the English language, on the subject of liberty, by the great economist.

Mills, William Haslam. *The Manchester Guardian, a Century of History.* New York: Henry Holt and Company. 1922.

An interpretative history of the great Liberal daily of England.

Nevins, Allan. *The Evening Post: A Century of Journalism.* New York: Boni & Liveright. 1922.

The history of one of the oldest and most highly respected dailies in the United States.

O'Brien, Frank Michael. *The Story of The Sun.* New York: George H. Doran Company. 1918.

A history of one of the most distinctive of American newspapers.

Older, Fremont. *My Own Story.* San Francisco: The Call, 1919.

An account of the experiences of the veteran Pacific coast journalist on San Francisco newspapers.

Park, Robert E. *The Immigrant Press and Its Control.* New York: Harper & Brothers. 1922.

A survey of the foreign language press, with data on the manner in which much of it has been subsidized.

Payne, George Henry. *History of Journalism in the United States.* New York: D. Appleton and Company. 1920.
An interpretation of events in the history of the American press in the light of contemporaneous political happenings.

Ransome, Arthur. *The Crisis in Russia.* New York: B. W. Huebsch, Inc. 1921
Examples of highly competent reporting in a difficult field, from *The Manchester Guardian.*

Robinson, James Harvey. *The Mind in the Making.* New York: Harper & Brothers. 1921.
A realistic account of the development of human thought.

Rogers, J. E. *The American Newspaper.* Chicago: University of Chicago Press. 1909.
A study of the space devoted to various kinds of news in newspapers fifteen years ago.

Rowell, George P. *American Newspaper Directory.* Boston: George P. Rowell. 1879.
An old directory, containing suggestions of interest on the publishing practices of its time.

Salmon, Lucy Maynard. *The Newspaper and the Historian.* New York: Oxford University Press. 1923.
A study of the excellencies and the deficiencies of the press as a source of historical material.

Scott, Walter Dill. *The Psychology of Advertising,* pp. 375–394. Boston: Small, Maynard & Company. 1908.
Results of a questionnaire on the time spent in reading newspapers.

Scott-James, R. G. *The Influence of the Press.* London: S. W. Partridge & Company, Ltd. 1914.
A discussion of the development of newspaper influence, referring chiefly to England, but treating the American press to some extent.

Shuman, Edwin L. *Practical Journalism.* New York: D. Appleton & Company. 1903.
One of the earlier works on journalistic practice, containing

material on the tendencies of the press at the time when the book was written.

Sinclair, Upton. *The Brass Check*. Pasadena, Cal.: Author. 1919.

An attack on the American press, which the author holds has prostituted itself to capitalism.

Stearns, Harold E., *editor*. *Civilization in the United States*, pp. 35–52, 381–396. New York: Harcourt, Brace and Company. 1922.

Essays on journalism and advertising, by John Macy and J. Thorne Smith respectively, as part of a general inquiry into American life.

Sullivan, Mark T. *National Floodmarks*. New York: George H. Doran Company. 1915.

Editorials, some of them on journalistic problems, from *Collier's Weekly*.

The W. G. N. Chicago: *The Tribune*. 1922.

A history of *The Chicago Tribune*, published in commemoration of its seventy-fifth birthday.

Thorpe, Merle, *editor*. *The Coming Newspaper*. New York: Henry Holt and Company. 1915.

Addresses at the 1914 Newspaper Week, University of Kansas.

Trotter, W. *Instincts of the Herd in Peace and War*. New York: The Macmillan Company. 1916.

An examination of herd instinct in its relation to contemporary civilization.

Villard, Oswald Garrison. *Some Newspapers and Newspapermen*. New York: Alfred A. Knopf, Inc. 1923.

A discussion of prominent American daily papers and editors, by the editor of *The Nation*.

Watterson, Henry. *"Marse Henry," An Autobiography*. New York: George H. Doran Company. 1919.

The journalistic and other experiences of the great editor of *The Louisville Courier-Journal*.

250 THE ETHICS OF JOURNALISM

White, Lee A. *The Detroit News: 1873–1917.* Detroi
The Evening News Association. 1918.
The history of a great Middle Western daily newspaper.

*William Rockhill Nelson, The Story of a Man, a Newspape
and a City.* Cambridge: The Riverside Press. 1915.
The history of the work of the late distinguished editor c
The Kansas City Star.

Williams, J. B. *A History of British Journalism to th
Foundation of the Gazette.* Oxford: University Pres
1908.
A work showing the restricted conditions of the press in th
seventeenth century.

Williams, Talcott. *The Newspaperman.* New York: Charle
Scribner's Sons. 1922.
A presentation of the opportunities and defects of journalisn
as a vocation.

Williams, Walter, *editor.* *The Press Congress of the Worl
in Hawaii.* Columbia, Mo.: E. W. Stephens Publishin,
Company. 1922.
Proceedings of an international journalistic gathering, in
cluding several papers on ethical problems of the press.

BULLETINS AND PAMPHLETS

Addresses and Proceedings of the Fourth Annual Meeting of the University Press Club of Michigan. Ann Arbor. 1922.

Biennial Reports, Bureau of Accuracy and Fair Play. New York: *The World.*

Constitution and rules, Institute of Journalists. Tudor Street, London, E. C. 4.

Constitution and rules, National Union of Journalists. 180 Fleet Street, London, E. C. 4.

Constitution and rules, Society of Women Journalists. Sentinel House, Southampton Row, London, W. C. 2.

Cook, Waldo C. *Character in Newspapers, University of Iowa Extension Bulletin* No. 62. Iowa City. 1920.

Ethical Aspects of Journalism, Bulletin of the University of Washington, General Series No. 101. Seattle. 1916.

How Confidence Began. Philadelphia: *The Farm Journal.*

How It Works. New York: *The Tribune.*

Lee, James Melvin. *Instruction in Journalism in Institutions of \Higher Education.* Washington: United States Bureau of Education. 1918.

Moses, Bert. *The Deadhead Reading Notice.* New York: *The Evening Post.*

Myers, Joseph S. *The Journalistic Code of Ethics, Ohio State University Bulletin,* Vol. 26, No. 8. Columbus, Ohio. 1922.

Powell, J. B. *Building a Circulation, University of Missouri Bulletin,* Vol. 15, No. 6. Columbia, Mo. 1914.

Proceedings of the American Association of Teachers of Journalism, 1921 and 1922. Minneapolis: R. R. Barlow, University of Minnesota.

Some Newspaper Problems as Seen in the State of Washing
    ton, Bulletin of the University of Washington, Genera
    Series No. 111.   Seattle.   1917.
Supplementary Lectures in Journalism, Bulletin of the Un
    versity of Washington, General Series No. 103.   Seattle
    1916.
The Better Newspaper, Bulletin of the University of Wash
    ington, General Series No. 81.   Seattle.   1914.
The Race Track Graft.   Detroit: *The News.*   1922.
Williams, Walter.   *The World's Journalism, University a*
    Missouri Bulletin, Journalism Series No. 9.   Columbia
    Mo.

MAGAZINE ARTICLES

(Chiefly since 1910)

Advertising and the Press. Nation 108: 1000–1001.

Allen, E. W. *Social Value of a Code of Ethics for Journalists.* Annals of American Academy 101: 283–286.

Allen, F. L. *Newspapers and the Truth.* Atlantic 129: 44–54.

American Society of Newspaper Editors Edition, *Editor and Publisher,* May 5, 1923.

And They Called It Journalism. Editor and Publisher, March 31, 1923, p. 34.

A Test of the News: Some Criticism. New Republic 24: 31–33.

Anderson, Maxwell. *The Blue Pencil.* New Republic 17: 192–194.

Andrews, L. O. *What Is News?* Sewanee Review 18: 47–55.

Bailey, T. P. *Orange Journalism.* Sewanee Review 27: 227–238.

Baltimore's Municipal Newspaper. Independent 74: 881–882.

Belloc, Hilaire. *Modern Life; the Source of Information.* English Review 1: 799–808.

Beuick, Marshall D. *The Psychology of Editing.* Quill, March, 1923, pp. 7–8.

Black, Ruby A. *What Shall Our Standards Be?* Matrix, June, 1923, p. 7.

Bliven, Bruce. *Newspaper Morals.* New Republic 35: 17–19.

Blythe, Samuel. *Pro Bono Publicity*. *Saturday Evening Post*, August 4, 1923, pp. 20–21.

Brant, Irving. *Press Is Serving Nation with a Poisoned Cup*. *Editor and Publisher*, December 9, 1922, pp. 5–6.

Brisbane, Arthur. *William Randolph Hearst*. *North American Review* 183: 519–525. See also editorial comment, p. 569.

Brooks, S. *The American Yellow Press*. *Fortnightly Review* 96: 1126–1137. *Living Age* 272: 67–76.

Brown, G. R. *Lynching of Public Opinion*. *North American Review* 209: 795–802.

Brownell, Atherton. *Publicity and its Ethics*. *North American Review* 215: 188–189.

Bryan, W. J. *A National Bulletin*. *Forum* 65: 455–458.

Burrell, D. J. *Wanted: A Newspaper*. *Marble Collegiate Pulpit* 32: No. 31.

Can Truth Be Enforced? *Arbitrator*, July, 1919, pp. 6–11.

Case of Mr. Hearst and his Newspapers. *Current Opinion* 65: 5–8.

Case of News Suppressed. *New Republic* 23: 8.

Censorship and Its Effects. *Quarterly Review* 25: 148–163.

Censorship and Suppression. *Nation* 104: 424–425.

Cobb, Frank I. *The Press and Public Opinion*. *New Republic* 21: 144–147.

Colby, F. M. *Sowing the Wind*. *Harper's Magazine*. 146: 384–391.

Colyer, W. T. *Obligatory Answers*. *Arbitrator*, July, 1919, pp. 12–13.

A Cooperative Newspaper. *Nation* 109: 454–455.

Crawford, Nelson Antrim. *Democracy Diagnosed*. *Dial* 73: 219–221.

Crawford, Nelson Antrim. *Mental Health and the Newspaper*. *Mental Hygiene* 6: 300–305.

Crawford, Nelson Antrim. *The American Newspaper and the People: A Psychological Examination*. *Nation* 115: 249–252.

Crucy, François. *U. S. Press Through the Eyes of a French-man.* Editor and Publisher, April 7, 1923, pp. 5 and 31.

Democratizing the Press. Nation 108:727.

Dreiser, Theodore. *Out of My Newspaper Days.* Bookman 54:208–217, 427–433, 542–550; 55:12–19, 118–125.

Duffus, R. L. *To the Highest Bidder.* New Republic 31:72–74.

Ellis, W. T. *Propagandists Feed New Fires of World Hate.* Editor and Publisher, September 23, 1922, pp. 5, 37.

Endowing Newspapers. Nation 107:60–61.

Ethics of Journalism. Spectator 109:161–162.

Every Man his Own Journalist. Living Age 311:810.

Faking as a Fine Art. American Magazine 75:24–32.

Fenton, Frances. *Influence of Newspaper Presentations upon the Growth of Crime and Other Anti-Social Activity.* American Journal of Sociology 16:342–371, 538–564.

Flint, L. N. *What Shall the Ethics of Journalism Cover?* Editor and Publisher, April 15, 1922, pp. 5, 30.

Ghent, W. J. *False Testers of the News.* Review 4:488–489, 509–511.

Gompers, Samuel. *Lying, the Barrier to Justice: Recent Strikes and the Public Press.* American Federationist 27:150–154.

Gompers, Samuel. *Oracular Editorial Writers.* American Federationist 28:309–317.

Griffin, S. B. *Journalism and Service.* North American Review 211:30–35.

Hall, H. *Hearst: War-maker.* Harper's Weekly 61:436–437.

Hamilton, W. P. *The Case for the Newspapers.* Atlantic 105:646–654.

Hanna, Paul. *The State Department and the News.* Nation 111:398–399.

Harrington, H. F. *Journalism as a Part of College.* Forum 67:476–484.

Hill, A. G. *Practice of the Kansas Code of Ethics for News-papers.* Annals of American Academy 101 : 179–187.

Holt, Hamilton. *Plan for an Endowed Journal.* Independent 73 : 299–303.

Hopwood, E. C. *Opportunity of the Press as a Moral Educator.* Social Hygiene 2 : 21–36.

Houston, H. S. *Working Out Business Ethics.* World's Work 28 : 384–388.

Houston, H. S. *Working Out Business Ethics.* World's Work 30 : 559–564.

Independence for Editors. New Republic 16 : 61–63.

Irwin, Will. *Age of Lies: How the Propagandist Attacks the Foundation of Public Opinion.* Sunset 43 : 23–25.

Irwin, Will. *The American Newspaper: A Study of Journalism in its Relation to the Public.* Collier's Weekly 46 : 15–18, Jan. 21 ; 14–17, Feb. 4 ; 14–17, Feb. 18 ; 18–20, Mar. 4 ; 16–18, Mar. 18 ; 27 : 18–19, Apr. 1 ; 2–22, Apr. 22 ; 17–19, May 6 ; 15–16, May 27 ; 17–19, June 3 ; 17–18, June 17 ; 17–18, July 1 ; 15–16, July 8 ; 13, July 22 ; 15–16, July 29.

Jones, Kenneth. *Journalism, A Branch of Commerce.* Fortnightly 1 : 826–833.

Kelly, K. *Newspapers and our Colleges.* Harper's Weekly 42 : 464.

Kennan, George. *The Associated Press: A Defense.* Outlook 107 : 240.

Lambuth, D. *Thinking on the Third Rail.* Independent 87 : 230.

Lawlessness and the Press. Century 82 : 146–148.

Lawrence, David. *International Freedom of the Press Essential to a Durable Peace.* Annals of American Academy 72 : 139–141.

Lippmann, Walter, and Merz, Charles. *A Test of the News.* New Republic 23 : sup. 1–42.

Lippmann, Walter, and Merz, Charles. *More News from The Times.* New Republic 23 : 299–301.

Lloyd, A. H. *Newspaper Conscience: A Study in Half-Truths.* American Journal of Sociology 27: 197–210.

Long, A. *The Federated Press.* Survey 45: 126–127.

Low, A. M. *The Modern Newspaper as it Might Be.* Yale Review n. s. 2: 282–300.

Mason, G. *The Associated Press: A Criticism.* Outlook 107: 237–240.

Mencken, H. L. *Footnote on Journalism.* Nation 114: 493–494.

Monopolizing the Press. Public 21: 593–595.

Newspaper Cruelty. Century 84: 150–151.

Newspaper Incitement to Violence. New Republic 8: 283–285.

Newspaper Invasion of Privacy. Century 86: 310–311.

News Writers' Union Local No. 1. New Republic 20: 8–9.

Ogden, Rollo. *Journalism and Public Opinion.* American Political Science Review 7: sup. 194–200.

Oklahoma Press Bill Doomed. Editor and Publisher, March 17, 1923, p. 18.

Opdycke, J. B. *The Newspaper and the Magazine in the Classroom.* School and Society 1: 832–838.

Paul, Edward. *Newspaper Methods.* Arbitrator, July, 1919, pp. 1–5.

Publicity Without Censor; Newspaper Reports of the Conference. New Republic 29: 29–31.

Rogers, Jason. *Don't Try to Curry Favor with your Advertisers.* Editor and Publisher, July 7, 1923, p. 10.

Roosevelt, Theodore. *Applied Ethics in Journalism.* Outlook 97: 807–809.

Rowell, C. H. *The Press as an Intermediary Between the Investigator and the Public.* Science n. s. 50: 146–150.

Russell, Charles Edward. *Applying the Ham Idea to Journalism.* Editor and Publisher, May 12, 1923, pp. 5–6.

Scholz, R. F. *Democracy and the Press.* Washington Newspaper 5: 135–146.

Science and the Press. Science n. s. 50: 347–348.

Scott-James, R. A. *The Great Experiment of Journalism.* *Nineteenth Century* 93 : 504–513.

Seldes, George H. and Gilbert V. *The Press and the Reporter.* *Forum* 52 : 722–725.

Seligmann, H. J. *The Press Abets the Mob: The Attack on Mr. Shillday.* *Nation* 109 : 460–461.

Sheldon, Charles M. *The Modern Newspaper.* *Independent* 73 : 196–201.

Shipler, G. E. *Freedom of Press vs. Freedom of Pulpit.* *Outlook* 108 : 774–782.

Slosson, E. E. *Science and Journalism.* *Independent* 74 : 913–918.

Stansell, C. V. *The Ethics of News Suppression.* *Nation* 96 : 54–55.

Stone, M. E. *The Associated Press: A Defense.* *Collier's Weekly* 53 : 28–29.

Storey, Moorfield. *The Daily Press.* *Atlantic* 129 : 41–44.

Swift, O. P. *Americans Find 439 Ways to Buck Censor.* *Editor and Publisher,* June 23, 1923, pp. 5–6.

Tainted News as Seen in the Making. *Bookman* 24 : 396–403.

Tenney, A. A. *A Scientific Analysis of the Press.* *Independent* 73 : 895–898.

Thomas, W. I. *Psychology of the Yellow Journal.* *American Magazine* 65 : 491–497.

Villard, Oswald Garrison. *Adolph S. Ochs, and his Times.* *Nation* 113 : 221–222.

Villard, Oswald Garrison. *America's Most Interesting Daily.* *Nation* 115 : 301–302.

Villard, Oswald Garrison. *Publicity and the Conference.* *Nation* 114 : 65–66.

Villard, Oswald Garrison. *The Baltimore Suns.* *Nation* 114 : 370–393.

Villard, Oswald Garrison. *The Kansas City Star: A Waning Luminary.* *Nation* 115 : 684–686.

Villard, Oswald Garrison. *The Monitor: A Christian Daily.* Nation 115: 493–495.

Villard, Oswald Garrison. *The New York World: A Journal of Duality.* Nation 115: 431–434.

Villard, Oswald Garrison. *The Public Ledger: A Muffed Opportunity.* Nation 116: 61–64.

Villard, Oswald Garrison. *The World's Greatest Newspaper.* Nation 114: 116–118.

Villard, Oswald Garrison. *William Randolph Hearst and his Moral Press.* Nation 116: 357–360.

Walling, A. S. *A Tribute to the Yellow Press.* Collier's Weekly 47: 27–28.

Warner, Arthur. *Enter the Labor Press.* Nation 112: 785–787.

What is the Matter with the Press? Forum 51: 565–571.

What the Public wants. Dial 47: 499–501.

White, P. L. *News.* Independent 108: 504–505.

Williams, T. *The Press and Public Opinion.* American Political Science Review 7: sup. 201–203.

Wood, Henry. *Ripping Off the Diplomatic Lid at Lausanne.* Editor and Publisher, March 3, 1923, p. 5.

Woodruff, C. R. *Municipal Newspapers.* Survey 26: 720–723.

Yarros, V. S. *Journalism, Ethics, and Common Sense.* International Journal of Ethics 32: 410–419.

Yarros, V. S. *Neglected Opportunity and Duty in Journalism.* American Journal of Sociology 22: 203–211.

INDEX